Britain
between the World Wars

Overleaf. Contrasting life-styles in inter-war Britain: *top* the rich watching cricket; *bottom* unemployed men tramping the streets.

Britain between the World Wars

1918–1939

Marion Yass

"The drums tap out sensational bulletins;
Frantic the efforts of the violins
To drown the song behind the guarded hill:
The dancers do not listen; but they will."
From "On the Frontier" by W. H.
Auden and Christopher Isherwood

WAYLAND PUBLISHERS LONDON

OTHER TITLES IN THE ENGLISH LIFE SERIES

English Life in Chaucer's Day

ROGER HART

English Life in Tudor Times

ROGER HART

English Life in the Seventeenth Century

ROGER HART

English Life in the Eighteenth Century

ROGER HART

English Life in the Nineteenth Century

ROGER HART

The Search for Prosperity: Emigration from England 1815–1939

RICHARD GARRETT

The British Sailor

RICHARD GARRETT

The British Soldier

MATTHEW HOLDEN

The English Aristocracy

MARION YASS

The Cost of Living in Britain

LEITH MCGRANDLE

Strangers to England: Immigration to England 1066–1949

COLIN NICOLSON

The Edwardians

CHRISTOPHER MARTIN

English Life in the First World War

CHRISTOPHER MARTIN

Crime and Punishment in Britain

J. J. TOBIAS

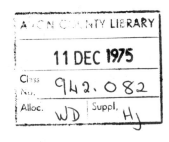
Copyright © 1975 by Marion Yass
First published 1975 by
Wayland (Publishers) Ltd
101 Gray's Inn Road London WC1
SBN 85340 431 3
Printed in Great Britain by
Tinling (1973) Ltd, Prescot (Merseyside)
(a member of the Oxley Printing Group Ltd.)

Contents

I *A Land Fit for Heroes*

The Armistice

AT FIVE O'CLOCK on the morning of 11th November, 1918, a train stood on a siding in the forest of Compiègne in France. In one of its carriages the British and French military leaders sat opposite their German counterparts. They had just signed the armistice which ended the First World War. A British aide telephoned the news to Buckingham Palace and Downing Street: "We then had a glass of port and went for a walk in the forest, which was wonderfully soothing after a busy night."

At the Front the soldiers, too, were relieved rather than elated. Only that summer the German armies had been surging forward; it was difficult to believe in a permanent end to the war. They had lost three quarters of a million of their fellow British servicemen in the four years of fighting; over two hundred thousand more from the Empire had been killed. A few officers with local leave celebrated in the nearest French towns; but reaction in the trenches was muted.

At home there was jubilation. The poet Siegfried Sassoon wrote that

> "Everyone suddenly burst out singing
> And I was filled with such delight
> As prisoned birds must find in freedom."

As the guns boomed out at eleven o'clock in the morning people abandoned their work in offices and shops. Crowds poured out into the streets to sing and dance. They celebrated on the open upper decks of the buses. Whistles blew and bells rang. Strangers kissed in the parks and in doorways; a nearly nude girl paraded through the centre of Oxford, cheered by the troops stationed in the colleges. In many towns the local police were directed to ignore the revelries unless life or property was actually in danger. In London King George V and Queen Mary made the jubilation respectable by bowing to the crowds from the balcony of Buckingham Palace. In Trafalgar Square a victory bonfire at the base of Nelson's column left a permanent scar on his plinth.

Revenge and Optimism

But hundreds of thousands of civilians did not join in the celebrations. They were mourning their sons, husbands and friends lying on the battlefields. Like the poet Robert Graves they had turned away from the revellers "cursing and sobbing and thinking of the dead." Many wanted

Opposite. Women of the W.R.A.F. celebrate Armistice Day in London.

Below. Returning soldiers greeted in London. Soldiers were promised "a land fit for heroes" but thousands were soon unemployed.

revenge. The politicians understood this feeling. That is why in the election campaign which immediately followed the armistice a Labour M.P., G. N. Barnes, announced he was for hanging the Kaiser; and Sir Eric Geddes, President of the Board of Trade in the wartime coalition government, told the Cambridge electors: "If I am returned, Germany is going to pay restitution, reparation and indemnity, and I have personally no doubt that we will get everything out of her that you can squeeze out of a lemon and a bit more."

While British politicians were making these promises to the electorate the twenty-nine-year-old Corporal Adolf Hitler was lying in a German hospital partially blinded by a gas attack. In his book *Mein Kampf* he later described his reaction to the news of the armistice: "We were to accept the terms and trust to the magnanimity of our former enemies. . . . My hatred increased for the originators of this dastardly crime." Leaving hospital, he described how he had decided to "take up political work." The feelings he described were typical of many Germans in 1918.

Desire for revenge on both sides was not a good omen for lasting peace. The Fourteen Points put forward by Woodrow Wilson, President of the United States, and accepted by the allies at the armistice aimed to "make the world safe for democracy" by prohibiting armaments, secret pacts, economic barriers between nations and by setting up a League of Nations. After announcing the armistice terms to Parliament on the afternoon of 11th November, the Prime Minister, David Lloyd George,

President Clemenceau of France (left), President Woodrow Wilson of the United States (middle) and Prime Minister David Lloyd George of Britain pictured in Paris during the peace conference, 1919.

hoped "we may say that thus, this fateful morning, came to an end all wars." He realised the danger of exacting the full costs of the war from Germany. At first he tried to warn the voters. But recognising the strength of their feeling and determined to lead a coalition government in peace as he had done in war, he succumbed to public pressure. In December he told electors in Bristol that "we propose to demand the whole cost of the war" from Germany.

During the campaign Lloyd George also promised to build "a fit country for heroes to live in." His optimistic belief that the pre-1914 world could be revived and improved was shared by most people after the armistice. Their mood was reflected in a cigarette advertisement: the wife says to her husband "Thank goodness it's all over now, Jack, we can settle down to peace and plenty." He replies "Rather, dear old thing; give me plenty of Army Club cigs and I'm at peace with the whole bally world."

Hopes for both peace and for a better society gradually dwindled. By their repressive attitude to their conquered enemies the allies encouraged the rise of the European dictators; a new Utopia at home was prevented by a combination of economic factors and unimaginative governments. Meanwhile, the electorate voted for the man who won the war in the hope that he could also win the peace. Lloyd George formed a coalition of 338 Unionists and Conservatives and 136 Liberals.

Adolf Hitler gained the support of the Germans by playing on the harshness of the victors' peace terms in 1919.

A man equipped with an anti-flu spray for spraying buses (1920). Influenza killed 150,000 people in England and Wales during the winter after the armistice.

Demobilisation

Demobilisation was the first priority of the new government. According to the scheme drawn up before the armistice "key workers" in industry were to come home first. As these were also the men who were the last to have been drafted the government was accused bitterly of unfairness. In the camps in southern England troops mutinied. They commandeered lorries and drove into London shouting "We won the war. Give us our tickets. We want civvy suits." So the plan was changed by the Secretary for War, Winston Churchill. Soldiers with the longest service were released first. For the next six months ten thousand men a day arrived home.

The returning soldiers found many changes, not least in their domestic lives. Their babies had grown into unrecognisable children; their wives had had a taste of working life in canteens and factories. It was as difficult for the wives as for their demobbed husbands to settle back into the old routines with comparative strangers. Consumer goods like clothes and furniture were scarce; rationing restricted food supplies, although it did at least guarantee fair shares for all. The physical strains of the war may have accounted for the vulnerability of the population to the influenza bug which now swept through Europe from the East. It killed 150,000 people in England and Wales in the first winter after the armistice; this was a hundred times the civilian casualty figures from enemy action during the war.

But the worst fears of the new civilians were unrealised: they had little immediate trouble finding work. They did not know then how short-lived the post-war economic boom was to prove or how many of them were to be out of work during the next fifteen years. The women gave up their jobs and returned home; the optimistic armistice mood encouraged continued investment in the old industries like steel and shipping which had been boosted during the war. It was the officers in their mid-twenties who suffered most; they had missed out on the usual middle class apprenticeships. Their elders interviewing them for prospective jobs had experienced little direct bombardment during the war; reports from the Front had, for propaganda reasons, been underplayed. They therefore had little understanding of the effect of months or years in the trenches on an applicant's self confidence. In his novel *England, their England*, A. G. Macdonell described the commandant of a recuperation centre, who "privately disbelieved in the existence of shell shock, never having experienced himself any more alarming manifestation of the power of modern artillery than the vibrations of target practice by invisible battleships."

Officers were expected to find work for themselves by using their contacts with friends and relations or to tide themselves over with their private means. Many sank their savings in unstable small businesses which would be unable to keep afloat in the bad years ahead. Something was done for the non-commissioned who could not find work. They were given free unemployment insurance while looking for jobs. A similar non-contributory scheme had been available since 1911 for workers in the seasonal industries of building, engineering and shipbuilding.

In one way, fears for their jobs helped the demobbed to readjust. In *England after the War* (1922) Charles Masterman recalled wartime predictions that returning soldiers "would never settle down to weekly wage-earning in the orderly ennui of man's ordinary peaceful day." In the event "the fierce interest of each of the majority was not contempt for his old job but fear lest he should be done out of it." And most workers in the immediate post-war years were not too badly off. Factory managements often provided cheap canteen meals and sometimes even free medical attention. For a while the insurance scheme proved adequate to cover those who could not find work.

Population Trends

Unemployment benefits slowed down a trend of the next twenty years. If an unemployed man knew his insurance benefit would enable him to survive for a few weeks he did not immediately move to another part of the country to search for work. Nevertheless there was a gradual move towards the South as workers looked for jobs in the new light industries. It was in the new suburbs rather than in the centres of the southern towns that they chose to settle. The largest increase was in the Home Counties around London: Middlesex, Kent, Essex and Surrey. Many regional dialects gradually disappeared as fewer people lived all their lives in the county of their birth.

The 1921 census shows that the population of Britain was increasing as well as shifting. There were nearly two million more Britons than in 1911, bringing the total to over 42½ million. The war had caused no ultimate fall in numbers: it had actually prevented the annual pre-war emigra-

tion rate of 300,000 which would have caused greater losses to the country than the 750,000 who fell in battle. The population increased by another two millions during the twenties. More people lived to be 65 and there were fewer children under 15. The working population was therefore increasing. There were also more women than men. In 1921 there were 1,096 females to every thousand males. The deaths of soldiers was partly to blame; but the main responsibility lay with the higher death rate in infancy of boy babies.

In spite of their numerical superiority, in spite of the efforts of the pre-war suffragettes and in spite of their contribution to the war effort, women remained second class citizens. The Representation of the People Act of 1918 enfranchised all men over twenty-one; but a woman had to be thirty before she could vote and even then could only do so if she or her husband owned property worth £5 a year. Votes for women over twenty-one came in 1928. It is surprising that the suffragettes did not then aim at achieving equality for women in offices, factories and the professions.

Class Differences

Women were in fact less liberated than their new fashions and manners made them appear. Similarly, the new simple fashions adopted by all women except the poorest tended to cover up another prevailing inequality in British society, the strong class divisions. The heroes returning

This was the reality of "a home fit for heroes" for many ex-soldiers, unable to find work.

11

from the war found no revolutionary change. Their hopes for a better deal in the country for which they had fought declined. So did their patriotism. A wartime sergeant major who had returned to his job as a bus conductor explained to Charles Masterman: "I don't see that it is my country. I don't own a thing in it." Lloyd George had promised a land fit for these heroes to live in; but over three-quarters of the population owned goods and savings amounting to less than £100.

It is true that the aristocracy and big landowners were hit by higher taxes and death duties. Many sold off parts of their estates, some their great houses. In 1922 *The Times*, under the headline "England changing Hands," described how one firm of auctioneers was offering 79,000 acres for sale. The Marquess of Bath sold estates in Shropshire and Hereford and 8,600 acres of Longleat between 1919 and 1921. The Duke of Rutland raised £1½ million by selling half his Belvoir estate. But such was the wealth of the aristocracy that in spite of these sales they remained the largest landowners in the country, secure in their position at the apex of the still rigid class system. It was the less wealthy landowners, the gentlemen farmers, who were more vulnerable. In his novel *Berry and Co.*, published in 1936 and set in 1919, Dornford Yates described how the owner of the estate of Merry Down had suffered from taxes and death duties. He emptied his stables, shut up his rooms and sold his family heirlooms. Eventually the estate was sold by auction. In Masterman's words, "Many smaller squires went first, almost unnoticed, passing from the homes of their ancestors to the suburbs or dingy flats of London or the villas of the salubrious watering places."

In the suburbs the ex-country gentlemen joined the middle classes, ranging from doctors, clergymen and civil servants to shopkeepers and clerks. Many had looked forward to retirement on their savings only to find that the rise in prices had cut their value by a third or a half. Those on fixed salaries were also hard hit by the rise in the cost of living. Interviewed by a *Daily News* reporter a schoolmaster described how his wife was forced to go "sticking" to save fuel, to take in sewing and grow rhubarb for sale in order to make ends meet. Nurses and general servants in middle class households were told their services were a luxury that could no longer be afforded. Between 1911 and 1921 the number of domestic servants per 100 families decreased in Liverpool from 13·5 to 8·3 and in middle class areas of London from 24 to 12·4.

Thus grew up the idea of the "new poor" in the suburbs. This was exaggerated. A large proportion of the middle class continued to live well. They bought new cars and other consumer goods, drank the new cocktails and sent their children to fee-paying schools. The double system of education did more than anything else to keep the class system intact. Life for the working class, the factory and transport workers and the agricultural labourers, changed more radically than for the upper and middle income groups in the next twenty years. Cheap household goods, the radio and the cinema increased the standard and quality of living, at least for the employed. But the lines separating them from the unemployed living in appalling conditions in the slums on the one hand and the middle class on the other were still distinct. So was another barrier in English society, that between north and south. While the

Daddy, what did _YOU_ do in the Great War?

A recruiting poster issued in the First World War. When peace came the slogan was used against those who had profited from the war.

standard of living rose in the southern counties the northern industrial towns were hardest hit by the depression. As late as 1937 George Orwell could write in _The Road to Wigan Pier_: "There is a real difference between north and south, and there is at least a tinge of truth in the picture of southern England as one enormous Brighton inhabited by lounge lizards. . . . In a Lancashire cotton town you could probably go on for months on end without hearing an educated accent, whereas there can hardly be a town in the south of England where you could throw a brick without hitting the niece of a bishop."

"Hard-Faced Men"

Because they felt insecure the middle class feared the workers. They also

13

First Newly-Rich. "It's a great secret, but I must tell you. My husband has been offered a peerage."
Second ditto. "Really! That's rather interesting. We thought of having one, but they're so expensive and we are economising just now."

A *Punch* cartoon (1920) commenting on the sale of honours after the war.

Stanley Baldwin, the Conservative Party Prime Minister who governed Britain almost continuously from 1923 until retiring in 1937.

very much resented the men who had actually made money out of the war, becoming the "new rich" while they felt themselves to be the "new poor." Suspicion of these men was widespread. The new members of Parliament after the post-war election were described by Stanley Baldwin as "hard faced men who looked as though they had done well out of the war." A popular song of 1919 made fun of the wartime recruiting poster, asking "What did you do in the Great War, Daddy?":

> "And all the profiteers who had lived so long in clover
> Fell a-sighing and a-sobbing when they heard the war was over,
> For they'd all made their 'bit' in the Great War, Daddy."

It was true that many businessmen had held office in Lloyd George's wartime coalition government. It was also true that many other businessmen who had won contracts during the war were able to buy themselves into the aristocracy: Lloyd George made nearly £3 million between 1917 and 1922 by selling peerages. So well known was the practice that Maundy Gregory was able to set up an office in Whitehall and extract £100,000 a time from naïve would-be barons, promising to acquire peerages for them.

Changes of Government

Gregory was not punished for his malpractices until 1933. Another swindler, Horatio Bottomley, editor of the journal *John Bull*, was imprisoned in 1922. He had embezzled subscriptions invited for the purchase of victory bonds, the interest on them to be distributed as prizes. The scandal increased anger against the easy money makers. Moreover, Bottomley, who continually talked of the "Germ-Huns" was—unfairly

—associated by the public with Lloyd George's attitude to German war reparations. The Prime Minister suffered from this affair; he was attacked over the sale of honours; he was becoming isolated in the coalition government. Abroad, the ferocity of the Black and Tans sent to quell the Irish rebellion and the failure of the Genoa Conference to solve the problem of reparations harmed his reputation. At home, the land certainly did not seem fit for heroes. In October, 1922, after Lloyd George's ill-fated effort to help Greece against Turkey at Chanak, Conservative leaders met at the Carlton Club. They decided to withdraw their support from the Prime Minister and the coalition. Lloyd George resigned and was succeeded by Bonar Law. Law had been the official leader of the Conservative revolt but Stanley Baldwin was the real instigator. It was he who succeeded to the premiership the following year after Law's death.

Another Tory leader, Lord Curzon, called Baldwin "a man of the utmost insignificance." But the simple unsmart exterior was deceptive. The new leader was a shrewd politician who managed to restore stable parliamentary government. Apart from the two Labour governments of 1924 and 1929 he governed the country almost continuously until his retirement in 1937, gradually taking over real power from Ramsay MacDonald in the 1931 coalition. In spite of the General Strike in 1926 and mass unemployment, politics remained unshaken by the communist and fascist movements of the thirties.

Ramsay MacDonald (left), Labour Party Prime Minister, and Philip Snowden (right), his Chancellor of the Exchequer, after their party was elected to office in 1929, for the second time.

2 Work and No Work

A FEW MONTHS after the armistice demobbed soldiers were busy in the factories, mills, mines and shipyards. Manufacturers were optimistic. They assumed the pre-war demand for British goods would revive. Unfortunately, the industries which had made Britain prosperous in the nineteenth century were less relevant to the twentieth.

Cotton, Shipbuilding and Coal

Cotton had been the most important pre-war export. In 1913 Britain had provided 65 per cent of the world's textiles. During the war imports of raw cotton had been restricted by pressure on shipping space. Many cotton workers left the mills for the trenches. The resulting shortage of clothes created an enormous demand as soon as the armistice was signed. Everyone wanted civvy suits and new outfits. Increased production was also boosted by the expectation that the pre-war markets would re-open. Businessmen paid huge sums for cotton mills, envisaging even more enormous profits. But home demand slackened as soon as everyone had bought their new clothes; and, more important, many previously British markets were now supplied by the Indian and Japanese cotton mills built during the war. Moreover, while these were equipped with modern machinery, little or no modernisation had been carried out in the old Lancashire mills. As a result of the competition many British looms were scrapped in order to prevent over-production. Nearly a third of the millworkers found themselves without jobs.

The shipyards told the same story. Before the war Britain boasted the most and the biggest yards in the world. Drawn into the war later than Britain, America and Japan both built up merchant fleets, creating modern shipyards in the process. Holland, Norway and Sweden also greatly increased their building capacity. By the time peace came all these countries were in a position to challenge Britain as supplier of the world's shipping. Orders placed in British shipyards were cancelled. Between 1920 and 1923 output was halved from a million to half a million tons of shipping. The shipbuilders joined the cotton workers in the queues for unemployment assistance.

Coal had been the basis of Britain's nineteenth century economic supremacy. In 1913 she exported a hundred million tons. Immediately after the war demand for her coal from abroad revived. But the demand

Below. In a cotton mill.

17

was temporary. French, German, Dutch, Belgian and Polish mines not only recovered but were modernised. Equipment in the British mines—as in the mills—was older and less efficient. Production was slow and expensive. Annual coal exports between the wars averaged less than half the pre-war figure. By 1925 one-quarter of Britain's miners were out of work.

Unemployment

Reliance on the old industries of textiles, shipping, coal, iron and steel had already been too great before the war; now it was disastrous. The wartime coalition, with no experience of the after-effects of a world-wide struggle, had seen no need for state planning or control of industry. When peace came Lloyd George did nothing to encourage alternative light industries. Instead, factories and mills taken over by the government for the war effort were sold off; steel works, railways and mills went back into private ownership. The enormous initial profits of the new companies encouraged private investment and speculation on the Stock Exchange. When the collapse came in 1920–21 many were forced out of business and their employees out of work.

Three-quarters of occupied people in Britain earned under £4 a week. These were the working class and they represented over 8½ million families. The majority worked in industry, others as domestic servants and farm labourers. As prices rose and the value of the pound fell, the

Gradual mechanisation on the farms helped make farm labourers unemployed.

middle class cut down on the number of servants they employed at home. On the farms mechanisation put labourers out of work; cheap food from abroad, too, meant that the acreage of wheat and potatoes increased during the war had to be cut back. The farmer's son who had left his Scottish village for London in *England, their England* was glad to have no more "anxious study of fluctuating prices of corn and turnips and potatoes, no depressing certainty each year that, whatever the weather or the prices, financial ruin was inevitable." While farmers gradually changed over to dairy and meat produce, the farm workers drifted to the towns at the rate of ten thousand a year. Between 1914 and 1931 the proportion of workers employed on the land dropped from $7\frac{1}{2}$ to $5\frac{1}{2}$ per cent.

The Dole

By December, 1920, over 800,000 men had lost their jobs. The figure rose to over a million in January and had doubled to more than two million by June, 1921. The 1920 extension of the unemployment benefit scheme introduced for demobbed soldiers was quite inadequate to meet this situation. Although it covered 12 million people earning under £250 a year, it did not touch agricultural workers or domestic servants. Moreover, the scheme now became contributory, which meant that those unemployed who hadn't contributed got nothing. Weekly payments were paid to cover the benefits of 15s. (75p.) a week for a man and 12s.

The "dole queue" was a familiar sight by 1920. This one was photographed in 1924.

(6op.) for a woman. Worst of all, benefit could only be claimed for fifteen weeks in any one year. The scheme had not been designed to alleviate anything but short-term unemployment.

In 1921 provision had to be made for men to continue to draw benefit even after they had used up their fifteen weeks' allowance. This benefit was paid by local Poor Law Guardians, not by the government, so the pressure was naturally greatest on those local authorities in poorer areas who could least afford to pay the benefits. It became known as the "dole." Being "on the dole" soon came to mean merely being unemployed.

The dole did not provide adequate means of survival. The usual rate was 15s. a week for man and wife and nearly 5s. (25p.) for each child. In 1920 the British Medical Association estimated that a family with three children needed 22s. 6½d. (£1·12½) for a week's food. As the man's maximum benefit was 30s. (£1·50) and his rent 6s. (30p.) even if he lived in a slum, this would mean nothing for fuel and clothing, let alone any entertainment. In Birmingham in 1921 a Health Visitor recorded in her case book that "Mrs J's husband's been out of work 14 weeks and there's five of them starving. . . . Although Mrs J was nursing her baby, I found that all the food she had had yesterday was a cup of tea at breakfast time, and tea and two slices of bread and butter, provided by a married sister living near, at tea-time." King George V wrote to the Secretary of the Cabinet, Sir Maurice Hankey, in the autumn of 1921: "It is impossible to expect people to subsist upon the unemployment benefit."

Wage Cuts

Not only the unemployed were in trouble. Many who kept their jobs found that their pay packets were being cut. Agricultural wages fell after the government announced it could no longer guarantee a minimum price for corn. Farm labourers received 28s. (£1·40) for a 50 hour week instead of 42s. (£2·10) for the 48 hour week they had worked in 1917. Cotton, engineering and shipbuilding workers were also forced to accept lower wages. When private owners received their mines back from the government in March, 1921, they terminated all existing contracts with their employees, introducing new lower wages. The miners had been discontented since the armistice had brought variations in pay instead of the national wage rates guaranteed during the war. A Royal Commission under Lord Justice Sankey had already recommended a shorter working day of seven hours, increased wages and nationalisation: "The present system of ownership and working in the coal industry stands condemned and some other system must be substituted for it."

Only the shorter day was implemented. When wages were lowered rather than increased a crisis blew up. The miners were supported by the railwaymen and the transport workers. The three unions had first concerted their policies in 1919. But the "Triple Alliance" was not strongly united. The transport workers' representative Ernest Bevin and the railwaymen's J. H. Thomas preferred negotiation to outright confrontation. On "Black Friday," 15th April, 1921, they withdrew their support from the miners' proposed strike.

So the attempt at workers' unity became known as the "cripple

An armoured car escorting
food wagons in London during
the General Strike, 1926.
Notice the buses driven by
civilians.

alliance." The miners, followed by most other workers, were forced to
accept reduced pay packets. The middle class was not immune: a 1922
Committee of Government Expenditure under the Minister of Transport, Sir Eric Geddes, cut teachers' salaries as well as introducing savings
in the army, navy, public health and most government departments. The
effect of "Geddes' Axe" was partly offset by a slight drop in the cost of
living. But in 1926 a Royal Commission once again recommended cuts in
miners' wages. This was too much. The miners refused to negotiate,
demanding in the words of their Secretary, A. J. Cook, "Not a penny off
the pay, not a minute on the day." This time the Trades Union Congress
supported the miners. On 4th May everyone awoke to a very quiet day.
The General Strike had begun.

The General Strike, 1926

Answering the call of the T.U.C. the railwaymen, the transport workers,
the dockers, builders, printers, engineers, the electricity and gas workers
all downed tools. They wholeheartedly supported the miners in their
claim that the standard of living achieved during the war should not be
lowered. A. J. Cook was jubilant: "What a wonderful response! What

A copy of *The British Gazette*, a newspaper issued by the government during the General Strike. Issues of the regular national newspapers were restricted as a result of strike action.

solidarity! From John o'Groats to Land's End the workers answered the call to arms to defend us, to defend the brave miner in his fight for a living wage." No factories opened; no commercial traffic filled the streets; no newspapers appeared.

The time between the setting up of the commission on the mines and the publication of its report had been better used by the government than by the miners. Plans were made for mobilising transport. Private cars would carry food from the docks to a depot in Hyde Park, then distribute it. The government was not short of volunteers for this work. Most of the middle class saw the miners as intransigent traitors willing to put the country to ransom for their own selfish ends. Professional men and university students enthusiastically drove buses, trams, lorries and trains. The tennis champion H. W. Austin was at Cambridge: "The greater part of the University rejoiced at the prospect of being able to help defeat the strikers. I went with a batch of undergraduates to help conduct buses from their depot at Chiswick Park. Unfortunately there were 600 of us all equally keen to conduct the same bus. We went to look for work elsewhere and obtained an excellent job on the railway."

At Oxford another undergraduate, future Labour Party leader Hugh Gaitskell, felt differently: "I hadn't been very active in politics before this but I knew that I could not possibly go and help to break the strike. I could not go and unload ships and drive lorries and try to drive trains as the vast majority of students were doing. I knew that I was on the side of the trade unions and the Labour movement." Gaitskell drove a car for the Strike Committee. In the middle class he was in a tiny minority. The General Strike was a class struggle. There was some violence: buses manned by "black" workers (that is, workers who ignored the Strike) were overturned; police cleared streets of angry workers with batons and in some industrial towns clashed with strikers. But the best recorded event of the strike was a football match organised by the Chief Constable of Plymouth between the police and strikers. The struggle was not bitter; and it was lost by the workers. If society in 1926 had been as dependent on technology and electricity as it is now the result might have been different. The T.U.C., by carrying on negotiations with the government, showed clearly they were not out to fight the class battle to the bitter end. After nine days they capitulated. The trade union movement became accepted as part of the social system.

Factory workers returned to their benches. More slowly, the miners went back to work, forced by hunger to accept longer hours and less pay. Worst of all, conditions varied from pit to pit according to the whim of the mine-owner. Exploitation of labour was made possible by the growing pool of unemployment. Nothing was done for the miners. But the General Strike did frighten other employers. No wages were cut for the next three years even though the cost of living actually fell. Most workers, until the Depression came in 1929, were better off than they had been in the past.

The Depression, 1929

The depression which hit Britain began with the Wall Street crash in October, 1929. During the twenties there had been unprecedented investment on the New York Stock Exchange. As the *Evening Standard* told its London readers "the speculative public includes artisans, lift boys, clerks and waitresses as well as businessmen." But the stock market bubble was blown up too high. When the recession came it burst. The worst effect on the outside world was the withdrawal of American loans from foreign countries. Not only could the European nations not now pay their war debts or finance reconstruction; they could not buy raw materials, manufactured goods or food from America or from each other. Neither could America, whose exports consequently fell, afford to buy from them. The slump was world wide.

As American loans ended, European governments began to withdraw their gold from the Bank of England. Britain was already suffering as much as anyone else from the recession. Her trading position had not been helped by her return to the gold standard in 1925: Winston Churchill, Baldwin's Chancellor, had been responsible for revaluing the pound at such a high level that British exports were more expensive than those of her rivals. Retention of another Victorian shibboleth—free trade—had also harmed the British economy. Just as their conservatism kept the British producing ships, coal and textiles in a world where there was little demand for them, so the politicians regarded with horror any government control of trade.

Now the second Labour government had to face the combined problems of the over-valued pound, the trade recession and world depression. There was a balance of payments deficit of over £120 million. Unemployment was still rising. Most politicians believed that unemployment would force wages down, thus lowering production costs; cheap industrial products would therefore be in demand, bringing increased employment. In the long run all would be well. Economist John Maynard Keynes disagreed: "In the long run we will all be dead," was his cynical reply. Instead he advocated expansion of the economy to provide more work. But neither he nor his only ally in the Cabinet, Sir Oswald Mosley, could persuade the MacDonald government.

Critics of government economic policy recommended that massive amounts of money should be spent by the government to provide work for the unemployed. Although some public works were organised—for example, road works (left)—the government rejected such a policy in general in favour of cuts in government spending and wages.

Unemployment and the balance of payments deficit both increased. By July, 1930, two million people were out of work; by the following spring the figure was nearer three million. Even those in work were having a hard time. In May, 1931, the economist G. D. H. Cole wrote in the *New Statesman* that "demands for wage reductions are now pouring thick and fast upon the Trade Unions . . . the railwaymen are restive under the reductions they have accepted recently . . . the chemical workers have been faced with a general demand for reductions." Cole pointed out that cuts in wages only reduced purchasing power. Mosley told the House of Commons: "These suggestions to put the nation in bed on a starvation diet are the suggestions of an old woman in a fright."

From the New York bankers came the ultimatum that unless the budget was balanced, no loan would be forthcoming. More particularly, the balance had to be achieved by a cut in the unemployment benefit. The Cabinet, which had been unable to find any answer to unemployment apart from the handing out of benefits, failed to provide a majority vote for this condition. MacDonald went to see the King, presumably to hand in his resignation. To everyone's surprise, Buckingham Palace announced that a National Government had been formed, headed by MacDonald and including Conservatives Baldwin and Neville Chamberlain, Liberals Herbert Samuel and Lord Reading and the two Labour ministers who remained loyal to their leader, Philip Snowden and J. H. Thomas.

But the economic crisis remained. In fact it grew worse when the fleet mutinied at Invergordon. In itself not a serious matter, the unrest shook the confidence of foreigners who withdrew even more gold from the Bank of England. The National Government was forced to take Britain off the gold standard. Nothing terrible happened. Labour ex-ministers complained "nobody told us we could do this." But instead of making the crisis appear unnecessary, the easy climb down from gold convinced the population that the National Government had averted disaster. In 1931 they voted it back into power with a blank cheque or "doctor's mandate" to cure the country's ills.

No new men and few ideas had been thrown up by the crisis. The National Government was merely a combination of the old men from all parties. Mild protection measures, the 10 per cent import duties bill and the agricultural marketing bill, went a little way towards stabilising prices. Encouragement of new industries brought some new jobs. In Parliament in April, 1932, the President of the Board of Trade, Walter Runciman, drew attention "to the new industries which have come to this country. . . . They include businesses like knitwear, ribbons, furnishing fabrics and other textiles, clothing, electric radio apparatus, leather goods, toilet products, paper."

The Means Test

In spite of the new consumer goods factories, no real answer was found to the economic problem. In February, 1933, there were over $2\frac{1}{2}$ million men out of work. As the queues for the dole lengthened, the benefits actually fell. Not only did the government make the 10 per cent cut

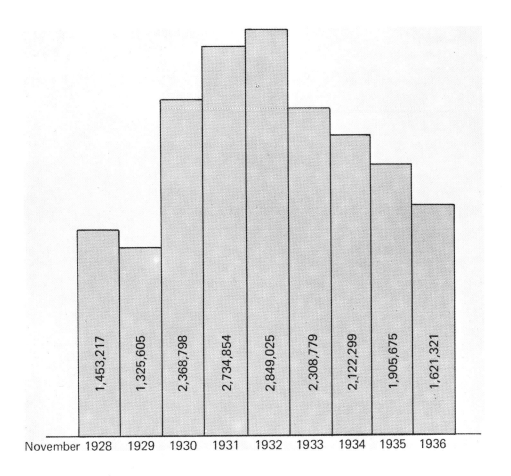

November 1928	1929	1930	1931	1932	1933	1934	1935	1936
1,453,217	1,325,605	2,368,798	2,734,854	2,849,025	2,308,779	2,122,299	1,905,675	1,621,321

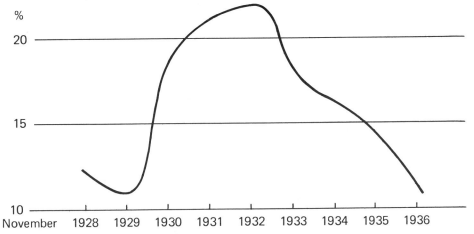

The unemployed in the United Kingdom, 1928–36: *top left* the total number of registered unemployed; *bottom left* a graph showing the high percentage of unemployed in the total registered working population.

demanded by the American bankers; they also imposed the means test. A man without a job was entitled to benefit under the unemployment insurance scheme only if he had paid thirty contributions in two years and only then for six months. His "dole" then became subject to the new test. As a journalist put it in the *Spectator*, "A new form of state aid was created for all thus excluded from benefit. It was drawn, not as a right, but only in proportion to the ascertained need of the applicant. Hence the so-called Means Test." Its aim was to cut local authority spending;

and every one of the new local committees set up to administer the test used it in a slightly different way.

The amount of dole given to each family was supposed to be related to the household's "needs." Officials visited homes, checking up on the savings and expenditure of husband and wife. Some even reduced the dole if a man received a disability pension or workmen's compensation. A child could not earn a few pence on a paper round or a working daughter accept a shilling rise without the amount being deducted from the family dole. In *The Road to Wigan Pier* George Orwell emphasised that "the most cruel effect of the Means Test is the way in which it breaks up families. An old age pensioner if a widower would live with one of his children. Under the Means Test, however, he counts as a lodger and if he stays at home his children's dole will be docked."

Benefits in 1934 began to be administered nationally by the Unemployment Assistance Board. Relief became "assistance" rather than the "dole." Local anomalies were eradicated but the means test remained. So did the psychological effect of a benefit considered not a right but in the tradition of the Victorian poor law, a charity. On his *English Journey* the Yorkshire novelist J. B. Priestley saw "men who, though they knew they were idle and useless through no fault of their own, felt defeated and somewhat tainted. Their self-respect was shredding away." Returning to England from Burma, Orwell noticed the same phenomenon: "When I first saw unemployed men at close quarters, the thing that horrified and amazed me was to find that many of them were

An unemployed man pays out his "dole" money to his wife, as his children look on. His dole is £2 7s. 6d. (£2·37½) for the week. The year is 1939.

ashamed of being unemployed . . . nobody cared to admit that unemployment was inevitable, because this meant admitting that it would probably continue. The middle classes were still talking about 'lazy idle loafers on the dole.'"

The Effect of Unemployment

Gradually the rest of the country began to appreciate the plight of the unemployed. The *Lancet* on 12th January, 1934, remarked that "the mass of middle class people are only now beginning to learn of the type of physical privation possible in depressed areas, where hardly anyone has resources beyond insurance benefit or relief." Their social conscience grew stronger as the thirties progressed. Meanwhile the means test added guilt to the everyday miseries of unemployment. The skilled man whose life had revolved round the shipyard, cotton mill or coalmine queued for his dole; he then sat at home or in his working man's club. If he went to his local pub he could rarely afford a drink or a smoke. A ship riveter's wife from Clydeside told a B.B.C. reporter in 1934 that in twelve years her husband had only had one year's work. They had had no holiday for thirteen years and her husband had not been able to afford one visit to a football match in all that time. They and their five children lived on unemployment pay of 33s. (£1·65) a week and a diet of bread, margarine and tea.

Young men who had not worked since leaving school were even more

The same man and his family have their chief meal of the day—boiled fish, dry bread and tea. The rent for their home is 14s. 6d. (72½p.) a week.

27

The Jarrow Marchers on their way to London, 1936. The aim of the march was to persuade the government to reduce unemployment in the North-East by creating new industries in the area.

apathetic and depressed than their fathers. They took the situation for granted, not even hoping for a job. Most depressed of all, probably, were the wives and mothers. Apart from the problem of housekeeping on inadequate benefits they had their husbands and grown up sons at home needing two meals a day. In 1935–6 Seebohm Rowntree conducted a survey of living conditions in York. He found that 31 per cent of the workers were living in what he called "primary poverty." This he defined as life below a line represented by the minimum sum necessary for the maintenance of physical energy. It was a standard of bare subsistence rather than an acceptable living standard. A family with four children living on 36s. (£1·80) a week spent 3s. 6d. (17½p.) on fuel and light, 2s. 3d. (11½p.) on clothing, 1s. 10d. (9p.) on household goods and 2s. 6d. (12½p.) on the burial insurance paid to avoid the horror of being "put away by the parish." This left after rent 16s. 10d. (84p.) for food, well below the sum laid down by the British Medical Association as necessary for an adequate diet.

Anger against the means test roused the unemployed out of their apathy. 2,500 of them marched to London in 1931 to petition against it. They were met by police with batons in Hyde Park and dispersed before they could deliver their petition to Parliament. Three years later the Labour M.P. for Jarrow, Ellen Wilkinson, walked with her 300 supporters through rain and high winds to see the Prime Minister who was visiting his own neighbouring constituency. Ramsay MacDonald agreed to see her. He could offer her no support except a promise to bear her cause in mind and the words which showed just how inadequate he felt himself to be: "Ellen, why don't you go out and preach socialism, which is the only remedy for all this?" By 1936 the unemployed shipbuilders of Jarrow were desperate. They collected funds to send a deputation the 300 miles to London. The 200 marchers carried a petition begging the government to introduce new industries to their area. After presenting it to the Commons, Ellen Wilkinson received empty platitudes from the government and a rebuke from the Labour Party for leading the crusade. When the marchers returned to Jarrow they received a cut in their dole money because they had not been available for work.

Increase in Real Wages

Rowntree had blamed the poverty of the northern towns on inadequate wages as well as on unemployment. Young men knew that if they did find jobs following their fathers into shipbuilding, textiles or the mines they would earn little more than the dole. But the worst of the unemployment and the lowest wages were confined to these old industries and therefore to certain geographical areas, particularly the north of England and South Wales. Some workers like the railwaymen and the postmen were always better off than others. Now those in the new light industries in the South were also receiving higher wages. Because prices fell even more than earnings after 1924, real wages for those lucky enough to have work not connected with a failing industry actually rose. The introduction of hire purchase and the availability of cheap luxuries raised their standard of living. Neville Chamberlain, then Prime Minister, told the House of Commons in April, 1934, that "the volume of our industrial production has very much gone up . . . I would say that we have now finished the story of Bleak House and that we are sitting down this afternoon to enjoy the first chapter of Great Expectations." He was a little over-optimistic. By 1935 there were still very nearly two million men out of work. Only rearmament was to bring the figure down below the million mark.

3 Sport, Stage and Screen

Football

ACCORDING TO an unemployed ship riveter's wife interviewed in 1934, the crowning deprivation of the dole was the necessary sacrifice of visits to the local football stadium. Watching the local Saturday afternoon soccer match was the most popular entertainment of the twenties. A million people cheered their own teams each week. In his novel *The Good Companions* J. B. Priestley explained why they did so. He described a road in his typical northern provincial town one winter Saturday: "A grey-green tide flows sluggishly down its length. It is a tide of cloth caps. These caps have just left the ground of the Bruddersford United Association Football Club. Many of them should never have been there at all . . . these fellows could not afford the entrance fee. When some mills are only working half the week and others not at all, a shilling is a respectable sum of money. . . . But for a shilling the Bruddersford United turned you into a critic ready in a second to estimate the worth of a well-judged pass, a run down the touch line, a clearance kick by back or goalkeeper; it turned you into a partisan . . . and what is more it turned you into a member of a new community, all brothers together for an hour and a half, for not only had you escaped from the clanking machinery of this lesser life, from work, wages, rent, doles, sick pay, insurance cards, nagging wives, ailing children, bad bosses, idle workmen, but you had escaped with most of your mates."

Soccer had become the national sport. Its popularity was not confined to the mill and factory workers. Gradually the middle class overcame its prejudice against the professional game. The Cup Final of 1923 drew nearly 200,000 spectators, one of whom was King George V. The new Wembley stadium could barely hold this number: the crowds surged onto the field after the match.

Cricket

Smaller crowds flocked to see the Test matches at the Oval and Lords cricket grounds. They eagerly awaited news from Australia when the British team played there. Newspapers carried terrifying headlines such as "Is England Doomed?" above their reports from Melbourne that Hobbs had been bowled for a duck. Hobbs and Sutcliff, later Hammond and Hutton, were schoolboy heroes. Cricket was less democratic than football. Neville Cardus, the journalist who almost elevated the game

Opposite. A favourite tennis star of the period, Fred Perry, in action against von Cramm at Wimbledon, 1936. *Below*. Two cricket heroes, Jack Hobbs and Herbert Sutcliffe, during the Third Test Match against Australia, 1926.

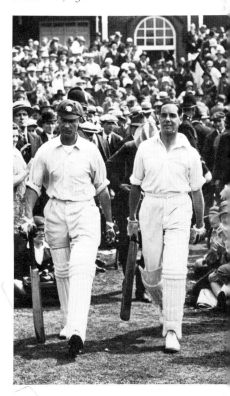

The popularity of soccer increased greatly in the period. Here police barely restrain some of the 200,000 supporters who watched the Cup Final at Wembley in 1923.

into an art form in his *Manchester Guardian* column, was read mainly by the middle classes. Schoolmasters and parsons used cricketing analogies, urging their pupils and congregations to keep a straight bat and play the game. County teams included professionals but the snobbery attached to the game demanded that the captain should always be an amateur. The popular annual fixture at Lords between the two groups was known as the Gentlemen *v.* Players match. However, cricket did have a wide appeal. Most country villages could boast a team. In *England, their England* the hero watches a typical game and describes "The blacksmith, his hammer discarded, tightening his snake buckled belt for the fray and loosening his braces to enable his bowling arm to swing freely in its socket."

Tennis and Golf

Not everyone had access to a local cricket team. But anyone who could afford a racquet and soft shoes might hire a tennis court in the park. Local authorities built courts in answer to the growing demand in the new suburbs, charging only a few pence an hour for their use. Shorter working hours meant they were full during summer evenings as well as at weekends. Lawn tennis—as opposed to the game of real tennis taken up by Henry VIII—had been played by the affluent at their clubs and country house parties since the 1870s. Now it became popular among all classes. Golf, on the other hand, remained a middle class game. The courses springing up on the outskirts of cities were inaccessible to public transport and their upkeep expensive. Only in Scotland were decent public courses provided.

As a spectator sport tennis also remained a middle class entertainment. Championships had been held at the All England Lawn Tennis Club

"The Arrival of the Jarrow Marchers in London" by T. C. Dugdale (1936).

Opposite. "Amongst the Nerves of the World" by C. R. W. Nevinson (1930). The painting shows Fleet Street, London.

Well-known artists were commissioned to design Shell advertising posters between the wars: *left* by E. McKnight Kauffer; *bottom left* by Brynhild Parker.

EVERYWHERE YOU GO

THE QUAY - APPLEDORE

BRYNHILD PARKER.

YOU CAN BE SURE OF SHELL

since 1877. After the building of the new Centre Court stadium in 1922, Wimbledon fortnight entered the diaries of the middle class as part of the summer's social round. Suzanne Lenglen first played there in 1919 and kept her title—except for one year—until 1925 when she retired after disgracing herself: she had kept the Queen waiting. Lenglen, Austin and other players like Bill Tilden and Fred Perry were given star treatment. They were hero-worshipped by the young secretaries and clerks playing in the parks and helped to increase the popularity of the game.

Traffic in Tooting, London on the way to the Derby (1922) All classes followed horse racing.

Racing and Betting

The middle class went to Wimbledon, the less well off to the Cup Final. Thousands from all classes attended the other most popular sporting events of the year, the Grand National and the Derby. Since the eighteenth century horse racing had brought together the aristocracy and the poorer classes in England: all loved to gamble. In 1928 the totalisator was introduced to race courses; in 1929 £230 million were paid out in bets. Many who could not afford the time or money for horse racing became just as keen to bet on greyhounds chasing mechanical hares. This new sport could be watched at night under the glare of floodlights in the 187 new stadiums built by 1932, an advantage shared by speedway racing.

Only the introduction of the football pools in the thirties really satisfied the national love of betting. On the elaborate forms filled up at home the football enthusiasts—and also those who didn't understand the game but wanted the thrill of a gamble—tried to forecast the results of the following weekend's matches. A lucky result could turn an investment of sixpence or a shilling into a fortune. For many the pools became an obsession. A Yorkshireman told Seebohm Rowntree in 1935: "A man

Opposite. "The Palais de Danse, Hammersmith 1921" by Therese Lessore.

33

Dancing the Charleston.

spends three days in considering next week's football, a day filling in his coupon and three days in keen anticipation of the following Saturday's results." During the football season the post office sold five times as many postal orders as usual.

The Dancing Craze

Crowds watched their favourite sport on Saturday afternoons; on Saturday evenings many visited their nearest palais de dance. These were large ornate halls built to cater for the current craze for dancing. The mythical "Jazz Age" began in England with the arrival in 1919 of the Original Dixieland Jazzband. The band's white players produced "jazzy" music rather than the real jazz of the black Americans in New Orleans and Chicago. But the new commercial music all came to be known as jazz; and it did have the same emphasis on the off-beat and the same technique as the original of imitating the human voice on the brass and reed instruments. The new music pepped up the waltz, the fox-trot and the one-step. From America came the shimmy, the quieter blues in 1923, the charleston in 1925 and then the black-bottom to enliven the repertoire of dances. A clergyman wrote: "If these up-to-date dances are within a hundred miles of all I hear about them I should say that the morals of a pig-sty would be respectable in comparison." In fact the dance halls were most respectable. Contemporary photographs show many of the dancers to have been sedate middle-aged couples. Compared with the later craze for "rock and roll" the twenties hardly seem particularly wild.

The new craze for dancing seemed to be a frenzied attempt to forget the deaths and miseries of the war. Most people believed there would never be another. They danced to the most popular tune of the time, "I

Wild abandon at a Saturday night dance in 1938.

34

want to be Happy," a hit song from *No, no Nanette*. If there wasn't a palais in the town, or if it was too expensive, dancing took place in any available wooden hut or village hall. At home the carpet was rolled back and the gramophone played until the older generation objected. For the more affluent there were the smart London hotels where the bands struck up at tea-time. Young women organised subscription dances to raise money for ex-servicemen, war memorials or Rumanians in distress. Dancing at meal times was first introduced at the Savoy. Tea dances were followed by dinner dances. Dining out thus became acceptable for women and a pleasant entertainment for all. Lyons Corner Houses catered for those who could not afford Soho or the hotels in London's West End.

Clubs

When the hotels and restaurants closed the dancers could go on to one of the new clubs with names like The Top Hat, Mother Hubbard's or The Morgue. These had sprung up in Soho after the war as a means of evading the licensing laws. Many were just one room with a rostrum for the band and a small dance floor crowded at the edge by tables for those who wanted to drink. The cocktail had arrived from America: everyone asked for a Manhattan, a Bronx, a Maiden's Blush or other mixtures often named after the barmen who invented them. The more exclusive clubs were decorated in lavish period styles and patronised by the aristocracy and foreign royalty. The Prince of Wales was a regular client of the Kit Kat Club. Best known was the Silver Slipper in Regent Street owned by Kate Meyrick. "The fabulous Mrs Meyrick" opened other clubs including the Manhattan where the American jazz king, Paul Whiteman, played. If one club was closed down for contravening the

The Seven Dials Club, London, one of many that sprang up after the war. The owner, Elsa Lanchester, is shown third from left.

1921 Licensing Act—no drink without food after 11 p.m., all glasses off the tables by 12.30—she would still have a living. In 1926 she was imprisoned for bribing a police officer; on release she opened the most famous club of all, the Forty-Three at 43, Gerard Street.

"Gay Young Things"

At private parties guests could drink champagne into the small hours, unimpeded by the law. There were fancy dress parties with national themes or invitations to "come as your ancestor" or "come as your dearest enemy;" bathing parties which shocked the public mainly because girls in swimming costumes—albeit with sleeves and legs almost to their knees—mixed with the black musicians; treasure hunt parties when the guests chased round London or the countryside looking for clues; and baby parties when they had to dress and behave as infants. Cecil Beaton described in *The Glass of Fashion* how Miss Ponsonby, the future Duchess of Westminster, "would, on an impulse, arrange a last minute party and ask her friends to contribute an essential ingredient: some benevolent godfather would supply a band, other guests provided supper, all brought champagne. . . . They had a splendid zest for life and ability for expressing that zest. Friends provided impromptu cabarets with their imitations and impersonations, elaborate and ingenious treasure hunts were arranged. The spirit of masquerade reached new heights, and almost every night there was some excuse for putting on fancy dress."

These were the "bright young things" whose antics—and adjectives such as "topping" and "ripping"—were copied lower down the social scale. They gave the "gay twenties" their name but were a tiny proportion of the population. Throughout the country many more pints of beer were drunk than cocktails or bottles of champagne. However, convictions for drunkenness gradually declined. Consumption of beer fell from 35 million barrels in 1913 to 27 million in 1920 and 20 million in 1930. The wireless or poverty often kept men at home; the greyhound track and the cinema offered alternative entertainment to drinking. Nevertheless, the public house remained the poor man's club. There he would play darts and dominoes. The gay young things were far removed from his way of life, from those trying to survive on the dole and even from the couples dancing at the palais on Saturday evenings.

Music and Theatre

So many clubs, dance halls and parties were fine for the musicians: there was always an opportunity to play in a band. At first most of the music played came from across the Atlantic. The most popular songs were nostalgic memories of American city dwellers—songs such as: "Back Home in Tennessee," "Alabammy Bound" and "Nothing could be finer than to be in Carolina." Gradually band leaders like Jack Hylton, Ambrose, Geraldo and Henry Hall became as popular as American Paul Whiteman; and songs from English revues entered their repertoires. C. B. Cochran staged light-hearted productions starring artists like Jessie Matthews and Gertrude Lawrence at the London Palladium. In *On with*

Left. "Gay Young Things" on
the way to a ball. *Above*. Part of
an Abdulla cigarette
advertisement showing a baby
party in the twenties. Guests
arrived in prams and wore
baby clothes.

"ASKING A POLICEMAN THE TIME."

A disapproving *Punch* cartoon
(1925) entitled "Ideas for Our
Bright Young People" (Notice
the Eton crop hairstyles of the
two girls on the left.)

the Dance, first staged in 1925, he introduced his "young ladies" and began the vogue for lines of dancing chorus girls. A Cochran first night was a glamorous social event; his most successful writer and collaborator was Noel Coward who allowed a note of disillusion to sharpen the romantic atmosphere the public obviously wanted. His most famous song was "Dance Little Lady" from *This Year of Grace*, produced in 1928:

> "Tho' you're only seventeen
> Far too much of life you've seen
> Syncopated child.
> Maybe if you only knew
> Where your path was leading to
> You'd become less wild.
>
> But I know it's vain
> Trying to explain,
> While there's this insane
> Music in your brain."

Coward also wrote plays making fun of the gay young things and the frivolous middle class. Elyot in *Private Lives* says "Let's blow trumpets and enjoy the party as much as we can, like very small, quite idiotic school children." There was an outcry in the press against the drug-taking son and immoral mother of *The Vortex* produced in 1924. John Van Druten's

Young Woodley about a public schoolboy falling in love with his housemaster's young wife received the same treatment. Other so-called "shameless" plays of the twenties were dramatisations of successful novels: Michael Arlen's *The Green Hat* starring Tallulah Bankhead in 1925, Anita Loos's *Gentlemen Prefer Blondes* and Margaret Kennedy's *The Constant Nymph*. Though such plays were outspoken they were sensational rather than socially committed. Only Ronald Gow's *Love on the Dole*, based on Walter Greenwood's best selling novel, dealt in a humanitarian way with topical social problems. The public had to wait until the production of J. C. Sheriff's *Journey's End* in 1929 for a play dealing realistically with the horrors of trench warfare. Bernard Shaw's *Saint Joan* —produced in 1924 with Sybil Thorndike in the lead—and *Back to Methuselah* only dealt obliquely with contemporary conditions.

The theatre-going public preferred escapism to realism. Producers understood this. They put on melodramas by the thriller writer Edgar Wallace, revivals of Oscar Wilde, *Charley's Aunt* and the fantasies of J. M. Barrie: *Peter Pan*, *Dear Brutus* and *Marie Rose*. In the thirties the most popular production was Terence Rattigan's farce *French without Tears*. The satires of W. H. Auden and Christopher Isherwood—*The Dog Beneath the Skin* and *The Ascent of F6*—showed less disquiet than the contemporary anti-Nazi plays being written in America by Elmer Rice and Clifford Odets.

Following the success of Gay's *The Beggar's Opera* in 1920 producers mounted a spate of Elizabethan and Jacobean plays. But there was no

Noel Coward and Gertrude Lawrence in Coward's play *Private Lives*, 1930.

Shakespearean revival in the West End. Shakespeare was left to two touring companies and a few repertory theatres in centres such as Liverpool and Birmingham where a modern dress *Cymbeline* was staged in the thirties. By then Shakespeare was left to the Memorial Theatre at Stratford and to the Old Vic under Lilian Baylis; she had also taken Ninette de Valois and the future Royal Ballet under her wing. Audiences for the plays which had been performed in front of all classes of people in Elizabethan times were now largely made up of intellectuals, American tourists and schoolchildren.

Music Hall and Musical Comedy

The real people's theatre of the inter-war years was the music hall and musical comedy. The latter was even less realistic than the offerings of the straight theatre. Spectacular productions were built around thin sentimentally romantic plots. The hit show of 1922 was *Lilac Time* at the Lyric. In 1926—the year after *No, No Nanette* opened—Edith Day as the star and Anna Neagle in the chorus began to sing and dance their way through 800 performances of *Rose Marie* at the Theatre Royal, Drury Lane. *The Desert Song* in 1927 also starred Edith Day falling in love with a Sheikh against exotic Moroccan backdrops. The next year's hit was *Show Boat* at Drury Lane. In 1928 and 1929 far more people were singing "Ole Man River" in imitation of Paul Robeson than were worried by the coming financial crisis. The most popular song of the early thirties was "You are my Heart's Delight," first sung by the German star of a revival of *Lilac Time*, Richard Tauber. *Lilac Time* was rivalled by the long running *White Horse Inn* at the Coliseum and then by three Ivor Novello hits at Drury Lane: *Glamorous Night* in 1935, *Careless Rapture* in 1936 and *The Dancing Years* in the last year of peace.

Music hall artists were even better known than Tauber or Robeson. At the Holborn Empire and the Metropolitan, Edgware Road, George Robey, Billy Bennett and Nellie Wallace provided more humour than all the great musicals put together. Moreover, these artists could pack up their acts and tour the provinces while the spectaculars were dependent on their elaborate scenery and revolving stages. Around the country George Formby sang "I'm leaning on a lamp post on the corner of the street," Flanagan and Allen rendered "Underneath the Arches," Will Hay performed his schoolboy sketches and Max Miller poured out his patter. Music hall generally was looked down upon by the middle classes as a vulgar form of entertainment; but they, too, loved Gracie Fields, the Lancashire girl who managed to be both funny and wholesome when she sang "The Biggest Aspidistra in the World" and "Walter, Walter, lead me to the altar."

Silent Films

Gracie Fields was one of the few music hall stars to survive the rivalry of the cinema. In 1931 she made a film herself, joining the ranks of the stars in *Sally in our Alley*. Her popularity coincided with the beginning of talkies; but the cinema-going habit had begun in the silent days of the

The music hall artist, Nellie Wallace.

A scene from *Lilac Time*, the hit show first performed in 1922.

The most popular star of silent films, Charlie Chaplin.

twenties. Before 1914 the British film industry had got off to a promising start. During the war it naturally lapsed. The Americans took over. When peace came the films shown in the small cinemas or "flea pits" sprouting over the country, like the jazz bands and popular songs, were from across the Atlantic. Hollywood produced stars like Ramon Novarro in *The Prisoner of Zenda*, Douglas Fairbanks in *Robin Hood*, Mary Pickford in *Daddy Long Legs*, Pola Negri, Dorothy and Lillian Gish and Lionel Barrymore. They became the idols of the British public. But one star was loved rather than idolised: by twitching his moustache or shuffling down a street Charlie Chaplin showed more emotion than any words could have done. *Shoulder Arms* in 1918, *The Kid* with Jackie Coogan in 1921 and *The Gold Rush* in 1925 established him as a great artist. Other comics— Harold Lloyd, Buster Keaton and the Keystone Cops—also made use of the chase, the custard pie sequence and the suspense situations suited to the silent medium.

The British film industry could afford neither the spectaculars, like *The Birth of a Nation* or *Ben Hur*, nor the star performers. The post-war slump meant that no backing was readily available to producers. In 1924 no film at all was shot in British studios. By 1926 only 5 per cent of films

Film stars Mary Pickford
(below) and Douglas
Fairbanks (right). The latter
is shown in *The Thief of
Bagdad*.

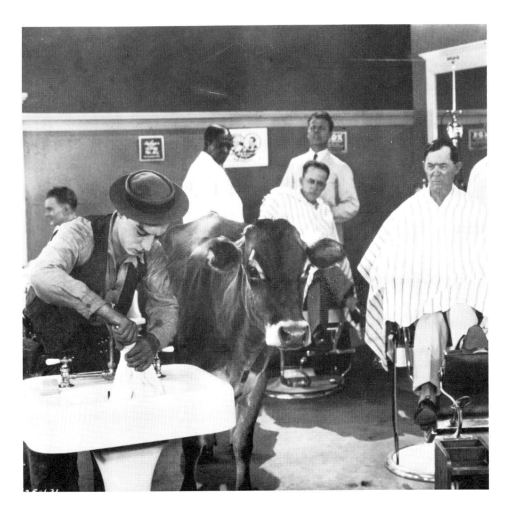

Buster Keaton in a scene from *Go West*.

shown in Britain were home made. But businessmen did put money into cinemas. The 4,000 flea pits of 1920 were obviously inadequate for the demand. More worthy homes were needed for the glamorous American stars and exotic spectaculars. New super cinemas appeared in London's West End: the Tivoli in the Strand, the Astoria in Charing Cross, the Regal at Marble Arch (now the Odeon) and the Empire in Leicester Square. Films were better presented and could be watched in the comfort of plush seats among chrome and gilt decorations. Below the screen was a platform large enough for orchestras twenty strong. The musicians provided music for the silent films. In less luxurious cinemas a piano sufficed: Gerald Bright played the incidental piano music for the silent cinema in the Old Kent Road before becoming Geraldo with his tango band at the Savoy. The new cinemas boasted giant organs which sank out of sight with their organists as the lights dimmed and the film began.

The Talkies

Organs and orchestras were made redundant by the talkies. If they couldn't find work in the clubs or dance halls the musicians joined the dole queues. Warner Brothers' *The Jazz Singer*, starring Al Jolson, was the first film from Hollywood to make use of the new techniques, though

A poster advertising *The Jazz Singer*, the first "talkie" film.

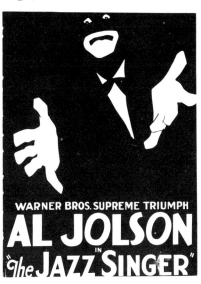

The Gothic splendours of the Granada, Tooting, opened in 1931 with seating capacity for 4,000. Many such cathedral-like cinemas were built in the period.

sound was at first allied to captions. It was shown at the Piccadilly Theatre, London in September, 1928. Jolson's second film *The Singing Fool* relied entirely on sound. Everyone hummed his hit song "Sonny Boy," but many were suspicious of the innovation. The quality of the early sound was naturally not perfect. Moreover, the novelty meant that directors lost the excitement and movement of the silent films, content to let the cameras rest on talking or singing faces. A. P. Herbert, writing in *Punch* in 1929, forecast that the sound film was "doomed to an early but expensive death." But the public was excited by the signs outside the cinemas: "100% All Talking Pictures" and, at last in 1930, "Garbo Talks." They needed little encouragement to go inside to see Gary Cooper in *Mr. Deeds Goes to Town* or Myrna Loy and William Powell in *The Thin Man*. In 1929 Walt Disney introduced Mickey Mouse in *Steamboat Willie*. Mickey was followed by Donald Duck and Pluto and, in 1938, by Disney's first full length feature, *Snow White*. In spite of the shortage of finance for British films, studios were opened at Pinewood and Denham. Alexander Korda proved the ability of British film makers by producing *The Private Life of Henry VIII* in 1934. Wendy Hiller, before going on to appear on the stage as the mill girl in *Love on the Dole* and to marry its adapter, Ronald Gow, co-starred with Leslie Howard in

Pygmalion. Alfred Hitchcock's *Blackmail* was the first British talkie; he was also the first to realise the potential of sound effects other than the human voice. The pounding rhythm of the train brilliantly increased the tension of *The Lady Vanishes*.

Popularity of the Cinema

Going to the "flicks" or cinema became the most popular form of entertainment in the thirties. A survey estimated that 40 per cent of the entire population saw one film a week, and 25 per cent saw two. By 1939 50 per cent had caught the habit. By 1937 Gaumont British owned 345 cinemas, Associated British Cinemas 431, and Odeon—founded by a Birmingham scrap metal merchant Oscar Deutsch in 1933—boasted 900. A further 3,000 were privately owned. Their names—Ritz, Majestic, Rialto, Astoria, Granada—glorified the suburban streets where they were found and provided a cheap and warm haven for the unemployed. George Orwell wrote in 1937 that "In Wigan a favourite was the pictures, which are fantastically cheap there. You can always get a seat for fourpence and at the matinee at some houses you can even get a seat for twopence. Even people on the verge of starvation will readily pay twopence to get out of the ghastly cold of a winter afternoon."

In the same book Orwell explained another attraction of the cinema: "You may have three-halfpence in your pocket and not a prospect in the world . . . but you can stand on the street corner indulging in a private day-dream of yourself as Clark Gable or Greta Garbo, which compensates you for a great deal." Most films were pure escapism. If working people appeared at all they were comic characters seen through the eyes of the middle class. Only John Grierson's documentaries had any connection with real life. But real working people were only too glad to forget the real life of the depression for a few hours. The cinema brought welcome relief.

4 *Reading and Listening*

Popular Fiction

POPULAR LITERATURE was as escapist as the cinema. Nat Gould's novels about horse racing were the best sellers of the twenties. As close second came the thrillers of Edgar Wallace who produced 28 novels between 1927 and 1930. His rate of output became a joke: people would ask at bookstalls for the mid-day Wallace.

Gradually the thriller was overtaken by the detective story. A young nurse working in a Torquay hospital happened to read a novel by Joseph E. Fletcher called *The Middle Temple Murder* published in 1918. She found it "excellent to take one's mind off one's worries." Agatha Christie decided to write a book herself. In 1921 she introduced M. Hercule Poirot, the Belgian detective, to the public. *The Mysterious Affair at Styles* was the first of a stream of detective novels to go on flowing for fifty years. *The Murder of Roger Ackroyd* was the best seller of 1929. Agatha Christie's example was followed by Dorothy Sayers who in 1923 added Lord Peter Wimsey to the ranks of popular detectives. He was joined in 1930 by Georges Simenon's Maigret—in translation—and in 1934 by Margery Allingham's Albert Campion. The genre was made respectable by the professional middle class: churchman Ronald Knox, historian G. D. H. Cole and his wife Margaret, and Professor J. I. M. Stewart under the pseudonym Michael Innes, all wrote popular detective fiction. To some extent they were writing—and their public were reading—as a reaction against the disappointment of their post-war hopes. They eschewed all mention of the unemployment, poverty and strikes around them. The public seemed delighted to forget such things and read instead about the aristocratic Peter Wimsey or P. G. Wodehouse's upper class best-selling hero, Bertie Wooster.

Libraries

So great was the demand for popular fiction—romance and westerns as well as thrillers and detection—that "twopenny libraries" had appeared in most towns by the thirties. Small stationers and tobacconists rented books from wholesale libraries, changed their stock periodically and charged twopence for the loan of each book. Readers did not have to join these libraries. They only lost business gradually after 1935 when Allen Lane, against all professional advice, began to publish Penguin paperbacks, selling at sixpence ($2\frac{1}{2}$p.) each. His first titles included Agatha

Opposite. Listening to the "wireless" in the 1930s.

Christie, Dorothy Sayers and Ernest Hemingway. Attractively produced in bright orange and white covers, they were sold on railway platforms and at stationers. Like the twopenny libraries, they attracted a new reading public.

For those more accustomed to the reading habit and willing to invest a little more in it, there were W. H. Smith's and Boots' subscription libraries. In the 1930s Boots bought over a million books a year; Smiths had three rates of subscription ranging from £1 15s. (£1·75) to 10s. (50p.) Volumes could be changed at any branch: those at seaside towns were busy in the holiday season. The subscription libraries profited from the fact that public libraries were both inadequately stocked and also considered unhygienic by the middle class. For the working class, however, especially for the unemployed, they were havens as warm as the cinemas. The Chief Librarian at York told Seebohm Rowntree in 1936: "It seems that while many new borrowers were introduced to the library through unemployment, the majority of them have retained the reading habit so gained."

Writers

More affluent readers paid an annual subscription of £5 for the convenience of having any book sent to them on demand from Harrods, the Times or Mudies. It was on these upper middle class readers that the sale of books depended until the coming of the paperback. Immediately after the war they bought and borrowed books by their pre-war favourites. Conrad and Arnold Bennett were still best sellers. E. M. Forster's *Passage to India* and John Galsworthy's *Forsyte Saga* were written after the war but looked back to the Edwardian era. In fact the literature of the intellectuals was almost as escapist as the detective fiction of the majority. Younger

P. G. Wodehouse, the creator of the popular upper-class hero, Bertie Wooster.

Authors of the period: James
Joyce (top) experimented with
the "stream of consciousness"
technique in his novel *Ulysses*;
Siegfried Sassoon (middle)
wrote vividly about the horrors
of the First World War in his
Memoirs of a Fox-Hunting Man;
T. S. Eliot (left) expressed
disillusionment with the times
in his books and poems.

writers seemed most interested in experimenting with style. James Joyce published *Ulysses* in Paris in 1922, though it did not appear in London until 1936. The "stream-of-consciousness" technique used by Joyce in that book was also employed by Virginia Woolf in *Mrs Dalloway* (1925) and *To the Lighthouse* (1927). Like Lytton Strachey and the rest of the Bloomsbury group she was exciting and revolutionary but at the same time out of touch with most people's real lives.

Only by the end of the twenties were writers and readers able to face the reality and memory of war. T. E. Lawrence's *Revolt in the Desert*—an abridgement of *The Seven Pillars of Wisdom* published privately the previous year—appeared in 1927; Siegfried Sassoon's *Memoirs of a Fox-Hunting Man* in 1928; Erich Maria Remarque's *All Quiet on the Western Front* in 1929 and, in the same year, Robert Graves' *Good-bye to All That*. The horrors of the First World War had receded; a second was not expected. The experience could be discussed. Indeed there had been such a surfeit of the subject by 1933 that Macdonell opened *England, their England* with the words "No-one need be afraid that this is a war book."

Only Walter Greenwood dealt directly with unemployment although others like J. B. Priestley, A. J. Cronin and Louis Golding wrote more realistic novels than their predecessors. The two most talented writers of the period, Evelyn Waugh and Aldous Huxley, preferred to produce brilliant satires on the upper middle class. They echoed the cynical disillusion of T. S. Eliot's *The Waste Land* (1923) and his *Love Song of Alfred J. Prufrock*:

> "For I have known them all already, known them all—
> Have known the evenings, mornings, afternoons,
> I have measured out my life with coffee spoons."

Like Alfred J. Prufrock, Lucy Tantamount, heroine of Huxley's *Point Counter Point* of 1928 saw no purpose in her existence. Living in a continual state of frustrated boredom she needed always to be the centre of activity, noise, lovers and friends. Her motto was "Living modernly's living quickly." Another character in the same book believed "that's what life finally is—hateful and boring." Boredom—the result of the dreariness of the factory bench and disillusion in a land which was not after all fit for heroes—accounted for the popularity of the escapist thriller and detective story. It was also responsible for the "crazes" such as for pogo sticks—long poles with cross-pieces for the feet and a spring on the bottom to allow a hopping movement—or for the Chinese game of Mah Jong.

Crossword Puzzles

The longest-lasting craze was the crossword puzzle. Collections of these puzzles in book form had appeared in the United States in 1923. One year later the first to be published in a newspaper appeared in the *Sunday Express* under the introduction: "Here is the great new pastime which it may be predicted with confidence will be the rage of England as soon as it becomes known." The prediction was correct. Most journals followed the example of the *Sunday Express*, the standard of the puzzle varying with

One of the many "crazes" of the period—indoor wooden horse racing.

the paper's readership. In 1930 even *The Times* succumbed. The crossword puzzle had become respectable, though still somewhat despised by the intellectuals. One of Huxley's most hypocritical characters was upset when found with his desk—where he was supposed to be writing his great work—covered in puzzles cut from the papers: "In reality Mr. Quarles spent almost the whole of his mornings on crosswords. They exactly suited his type of intelligence."

Competing Newspapers

Competition in the newspaper world had forced *The Times* to satisfy its readers' demand for crossword puzzles. For the twenties and thirties were the years of warfare in Fleet Street. Alfred Harmsworth, the first great newspaper baron Lord Northcliffe, died in 1922. His *Times* was now bought by the younger son of Lord Astor and edited by Geoffrey Dawson. It kept its position as the accepted journal of authority among the professional classes. Businessmen preferred the *Morning Post* which was absorbed into the *Daily Telegraph* in 1937. More liberal-minded readers bought the *Daily News* or the *Daily Chronicle*; in 1930 these merged into the anti-Conservative *News Chronicle*.

Northcliffe (left) and
Rothermere—together they
boosted the sales of the *Daily
Mail* by popular news
presentation.

The real battle for mass-readership was waged between the popular papers. Northcliffe had revolutionised the *Daily Mail* by his news presentation. Gone were the long dreary political reports. Instead there were short, snappy summaries of speeches and full reports of sporting events. The public loved this recipe and sales soared: Northcliffe's brother Lord Rothermere inherited a newspaper which actually made a profit. On its front page it boasted: "*Daily Mail*, one million sale." The *Mail*'s closest rival in the twenties was the *Daily Express* bought by Max Aitken, later Lord Beaverbrook, in 1916 to forward his belief in Empire free trade. Then, in 1929, J. S. Elias of the Odhams publishing group took over the *Daily Herald* with financial backing from the T.U.C.

Being a businessman Elias, later Lord Southwood, applied business methods to selling his paper. He introduced a series of simple competitions with large cash prizes and paid an army of canvassers to publicise them by knocking on doors. Luckily for him there were 50,000 unemployed articulate men only too willing to do this job for £3 a week. Soon the *Herald* was offering not only competition prizes to its readers but, if they registered their order with the publisher, free copies of *Home Doctor*, *Handyman* and complete sets of Dickens. Naturally, its rivals followed suit, promising cameras, tea sets, kettles, fountain pens, watches, ladies underwear and more volumes of Dickens. Whether or not more people read newspapers in the thirties, more certainly bought them. By 1939 the *Daily Express* had won the circulation battle with nearly $2\frac{1}{2}$ million copies, the *Daily Herald* sold 2 million, the *Daily Mail* just over and the *News Chronicle* just under $1\frac{1}{2}$ million.

The success of the *Daily Express* was partly due to its appeal to all classes rather than to a particular section of the public; but also to its lively presentation and the ability of its journalists to produce scoops. It did not take serious news too seriously, preferring to keep its readers happy. They were told what they wanted to hear, especially that no war was imminent. The popular press became trivial. By the end of the thirties the *Daily Mirror* had introduced the big black headlines and the nearly nude girls—including Jane of the cartoon serial—which were to win the circulation battle during the real war to come.

Newspapers were run by business tycoons, not professional journalists. Some had political ambitions. Beaverbrook and Rothermere both thought they could deliver the votes of their readers; they believed they were in a position to blackmail the government because they gave so many people their daily reading matter. But Baldwin was right when he accused them in 1931 of aiming at "power without responsibility—the prerogative of the harlot throughout the ages." For the press lords were less interested in creating responsible public opinion than in increasing their circulations in order to attract advertising. The public were not helped by their newspapers to form considered judgments and therefore to criticise and influence the government of the country; instead they were offered scandals, sensations, racing tips and crosswords.

Lord Beaverbrook, owner of the *Daily Express*, which had won the circulation battle by 1939 with nearly 2½ million copies a day. Beaverbrook and Rothermere were accused by Baldwin of using their powers as newspaper owners for political ends.

Radio

One reason for the bias of the press towards entertainment was the influence of the radio. Radio, or the "wireless" as it was called, arrived in 1922, the year Rothermere inherited the *Daily Mail* from Northcliffe. Regular news bulletins, read in London, were broadcast simultaneously from all regional stations. To be first with the news was now impossible for newspaper editors. They printed earlier, leaving the late night news to radio, and concentrated on achieving a wider distribution over the country. Presentation of the news was forced to become more lively to compete with the immediacy of radio; it often became sensational.

In 1926 the British Broadcasting Company was transformed into the British Broadcasting Corporation. At the same time John Reith, the managing director of the Company who had answered an advertisement for a general manager in 1922, was transformed into Sir John (later Lord) Reith. As Director General of the new Corporation Reith, mindful of his Presbyterian upbringing, believed that broadcasting should be conducted "as a public service with definite standards . . . not used for entertainment purposes alone. . . . The preservation of a high moral tone is obviously of paramount importance." Only broadcasting under unified control would be able to maintain consistently high standards. The Post Office, the licensing authority for wireless stations, in any case found it too complicated to choose between the various contenders for the stations: the B.B.C. became a monopoly.

Lord Reith, first Director-General of the B.B.C. He insisted on the importance "of a high moral tone" in broadcasting.

Listening to the radio was at first not a simple pleasure. It involved crystal sets, "cats' whiskers", ear-phones, aerials and everyone else in the house keeping quiet. Soon the valve-set surmounted by a loudspeaker enabled the whole family to listen at once. In the thirties the wireless became a large piece of furniture incorporating the loudspeaker. It dominated the living room as the television does today. Apart from the

Above. Listening to a crystal set in 1924. *Right.* Broadcasting Shakespeare in 1923.

regular news bulletins, the family listened to *Women's Hour* at two o'clock, *Children's Hour* at five o'clock, Marion Cran on gardening, Desmond MacCarthy the literary critic on books and James Agate on the theatre. *Children's Hour* was introduced by a series of "uncles" and "aunts;" all programmes had an avuncular middle class flavour. During the General Strike in 1926 all news the government did not want published was suppressed.

Reith believed broadcasting "should bring into the greatest possible number of homes all that is best in every department of human knowledge, endeavour and achievement." The B.B.C. was to be not only the moral guardian of the people but also their educator. And it did educate the public, especially in an appreciation of classical music. Sir Walford Davies, master of the King's Musick, talked about musical theory, Christopher Stone about the new classical records just appearing. Sir Henry Wood's promenade concerts were run by the B.B.C. after 1927; in 1930 the Corporation acquired its own symphony orchestra.

Reith filled the air with religious broadcasts. Ironically, the daily services, the morning and evening services, the Sunday night epilogues and the seasonal devotional talks probably brought such a surfeit of religion into the home that many people stopped going to church (see Chapter 8). But some fun was allowed into Broadcasting House. Radio's first comic was John Henry whose regular opening words became a catchphrase: "This is Gillie Potter speaking to you in basic English." He was followed by Arthur Askey, Richard Murdoch and Tommy Handley, though the latter only made his name during the war. Nor was the musical output all solemn. While Adrian Boult conducted the symphony orchestra, Jack Payne led the B.B.C. dance orchestra late into the night so that the

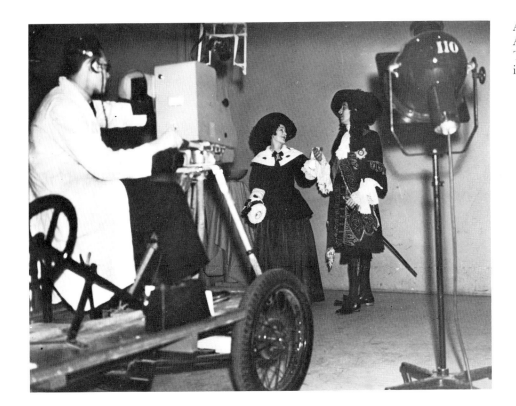

A B.B.C. television studio at
Alexandria Palace, 1938.
Television transmissions started
in 1936.

dancing craze could be carried into the home. Seebohm Rowntree's
survey showed that in York the radio was mainly used by housewives for
"company" when at home alone and for light music during meal times,
for light entertainment and news. Voices of politicians also became part
of domestic life. Stanley Baldwin was the first Prime Minister to broadcast to the nation. His relaxed intimate style was far more suited to the
medium than the oratory of Lloyd George or Ramsay MacDonald who
had less success on the air. Political leaders and issues were brought closer
to people's lives than ever before. The political importance of the radio in
controlling the public was first realised during the General Strike and
accepted by the time of the Abdication Crisis (see Chapter 8).

Between 1929 and 1933 the Post Office doubled the sale of radio
licences; by 1939 three families out of four owned a wireless set. In 1936
the B.B.C. opened its first television service from Alexandra Palace but
by the beginning of the war there were only 50,000 viewers. The influence of radio only diminished with the development of television after
the war. Meanwhile the radio, like the cinema and then the paperback,
brought a whole new culture to many who had previously had very little
culture of any kind.

5 Transport

Motor Cars

BEFORE THE WAR the motor car had been the new plaything of the rich. Wealthy men owned Lanchesters, Daimlers and Rileys and went to the 1909 motor show to see the new Rolls Royce "Silver Cloud." By 1913 there were 198 different cars on the market. Each example of every model was individually made in the factory. The war did nothing to encourage mass production, for mechanised transport was never wholeheartedly adopted by the army. When the demobbed soldiers returned home they found one cab in every ten still drawn by a horse.

There was one cheap car available, the "Tin Lizzie" or Model-T Ford. Its mass-produced American parts were imported, then assembled at Manchester. Import duties on the Ford encouraged British manufacturers to compete. At his Oxford and Cowley factories William Morris—later Lord Nuffield—produced family cars. Although they were more expensive than the Tin Lizzie, the Morris Oxford and the Morris Cowley saloons rivalled the uglier box-like Ford in popularity. By 1924 the Cowley two-seater cost £198 and the Tin Lizzie £125. Meanwhile Sir Herbert Austin, knighted for making guns during the war, used his idle factories for producing a car that was small, cheap, yet able to carry four passengers in comfort. The Baby Austin appeared in 1922 followed by the early Morris Minor. Their success was due partly to the new mass-production methods first introduced into the Morris Birmingham factory in 1923 and partly to the low taxation on low horse-powered cars.

Opposite. A traffic jam in London, 1928. By 1925 jams in the cities had become a serious problem.
Left. A Daimler in 1921. It was hand-built, as were most cars in the early twenties.

The large sales of such cars as the Austin Seven (above) were achieved because mass production brought the prices down to within reach of a mass market. *Right.* Mass production at the Morris factory.

In 1922 about one family out of 30 owned a car; by 1927 one in every 12. Nearly 200,000 cars on British roads in 1920 had multiplied to over a million by 1930. By 1939 there would be nearly two million. In the early twenties they were outnumbered by motor cycles. In fact it was their popularity which inspired the birth of the Austin Seven: Herbert Austin determined the size of his Baby by measuring the height, width and length of the space taken up by his foreman's B.S.A. motor cycle and sidecar. Many of these motor cycles were bought by ex-servicemen with their demobilisation grants. They carried their girl friends on their "flapper brackets" or pillions.

Country people hated the cars and motor cycles which dashed through the narrow lanes bringing noise, fumes and danger. Previously isolated villagers came to dread the invasion of picnickers on summer Sundays with the attendant horrors of empty bottles and waste paper. Often they encouraged their children to throw stones at passing cars or to scatter nails and broken glass on the roads. A rift opened between pedestrians and car owners. The majority still considered motoring a dangerous sport rather than a useful method of getting about. The sport itself was so frowned upon that motor racing was allowed only at the Brooklands track until Donnington Park opened in 1933.

Cars were mainly reserved for the jaunt to the country or for visiting friends. Few motorists used their Tin Lizzies, Baby Austins or Morris Oxfords for the daily journey to work and back. Nevertheless, the first traffic jams were beginning to block the centres of towns and cities. Commercial vehicles, lorries and vans, were used for deliveries of all

The 14/45 H.P. **ROVER** FOUR-FIVE SEATER MODEL

For Motoring Enjoyment—Choose a Rover!

Built of proved material by skilled craftsmen, all-British Rover Cars offer perfection in detail and utter reliability. There are two types: 9/20 h.p. from £185, and 14/45 h.p. from £550. Full particulars with pleasure.

THE ROVER COMPANY, Ltd., COVENTRY.

At first cars were mainly used for pleasure. This advertisement of 1926 reflects such use.

59

Carefree, crash-helmet-free youth in the 1930s. In the early 1920s motor cycles outnumbered motor cars.

Herbert Morrison, Minister of Transport in the second Labour government. He devised the London Passenger Transport Board to control London's bus services. It replaced competing private companies.

kinds. While there were under 200,000 cars in 1920, there were 650,000 licenced motor vehicles. Any picture of central London in the twenties shows the roads clogged with taxis and the new motor buses. These double deckers were at first open to the wind and rain. Tarpaulin covers were provided to cover laps and legs. In 1925 such discomforts were eliminated by the first roofed double deckers. The London General Omnibus Company under Lord Ashfield, an ex-President of the Board of Trade, operated most of the buses. But the routes were also served by small private companies whose so-called "pirate" buses tried to operate just ahead of the "Generals" in order to pick up fares. As rival drivers spotted potential passengers—specially designated bus stops came later —they wove through the traffic in a race to the kerb, often barely averting collision.

Buses

By employing the growing numbers of unemployed men willing to drive and conduct their buses for low wages, the pirate companies were able to cut their fares. Ashfield demanded legislation for a "protected monopoly" but met his match in Herbert Morrison, the Labour government's Minister of Transport. The London Passenger Transport Board was devised by Morrison and created by the National Government in 1933. Ashfield lost his private monopoly but became chairman of the new Board; the pirates were eliminated. Outside London existing operators were protected by the licensing system also introduced by Morrison.

Buses dominated the London streets because in 1872 a veto had been passed against the laying down of additional tramlines in the city. In most other towns, public transport meant trams. They could carry up to eighty people, were cheap and reliable. Their numbers increased during the twenties until there were 14,000 operating over 2,600 miles; but they

were doomed by the motor car. Every time a tram stopped on its tracks in the middle of the road to pick up passengers, the traffic behind it was held up. If vans and cars attempted to pass on the inside the lives of those alighting were endangered. In 1931 a Royal Commission recommended that no more tramways should be constructed and existing ones gradually removed. By 1932 buses were carrying more passengers than trams.

Some towns, including London, introduced trolley buses. They ran on electric power using overhead wires instead of tracks, and were quieter and more comfortable than the old trams. But while the long arms reaching to the wires enabled the trolley driver to pull into the kerb to pick up his passengers, they so often lost contact that traffic jams increased while the necessary repairs were made. In spite of their advantages they could not compete with the motor bus.

Until 1933 motor racing was so frowned upon that it was only allowed at Brooklands (above).

Traffic Jams and Road Accidents

By the mid-twenties traffic congestion in the large towns had become a real problem. One day in 1925 cars, taxis and buses in the Strand, London, were unable to move for two hours. Some sort of planning and control was obviously necessary. Roundabouts were introduced the following year in Piccadilly Circus, Trafalgar Square, Parliament Square and Hyde Park Corner. Narrow side streets were designated as one-way routes. Policemen were finding it impossible to control the growing volume of traffic at busy crossings. Traffic lights came first to Wolverhampton in 1927, then to Edinburgh and Leeds. Then the first London signals appeared in St. James's Street.

Motorists were frustrated by hold ups, but pedestrians were being knocked down. Anyone could buy a car, get in and drive it. Until 1931 he did not even have to sign a declaration of physical fitness. Naturally there were mishaps. In fact the accident rate was higher in 1934 than in 1963.

A tram on a Lancashire road. In most towns outside London trams were the main form of public transport until they were phased out in the early thirties.

61

Right. An accident involving a pedestrian and taxi in 1925. Until 1931 anyone could buy a car and drive it. This contributed to the high accident rate.

Opposite top. Piccadilly Circus in 1925. In 1926 a roundabout system was introduced here and at other busy junctions where police (seen in the picture) were finding traffic control impossible. *Opposite bottom.* Traffic signals were introduced in London at the end of the 1920s. This is Trafalgar Square in 1934.

"Safety First" campaigns started in the press. Advice was given to pedestrians not to read newspapers when crossing roads and not to drop parcels in the middle of busy streets. Something more stringent was needed. In 1930 Morrison passed the Road Traffic Act through Parliament. It introduced the Highway Code and compulsory third party insurance; local authorities were given powers to make streets into one-way routes and set up roundabouts and road signs. Actual safety regulations were, however, minimal: motor cyclists were forbidden to carry more than one pillion rider; lorry and bus drivers were limited to a certain number of hours on the road without a rest; tougher penalties were introduced for dangerous driving; but the old 20 m.p.h. speed limit was abolished. The *Morning Post* described the Act as "a great charter for the ordered use of the King's Highway;" but it was not until 1934 that driving tests and the 30 m.p.h. speed limit at last made the roads relatively safe. Leslie Hore-Belisha was the Minister of Transport in the National Government responsible for the new legislation and for the Belisha beacons placed at either end of the new pedestrian crossings.

The "Tube"

By the mid-twenties Londoners were already able to avoid traffic jams by travelling underground. Lord Ashfield had been king of the tubes as well as the buses, and had merged the early underground lines into a combine. This, too, was taken over, under his own chairmanship, by the Passenger Transport Board in 1933. One of the motives for the formation of the Board was the ability of the profitable buses to cover the losses of the expensive tubes. In 1924 the Hampstead tube line was extended to Hendon and Edgware. The President of the Board of Trade switched on the current with a golden key; his ten year old son then drove the first

Londoners could escape the traffic jams by travelling on the underground railway (right). As the lines were extended out of London (below) the older lines were modernized.

FROM EUSTON TO CLAPHAM COMMON
THE TRANSFORMATION
IS COMPLETE

train through the new tunnel which soon emerged into the open country of Middlesex. The City line reached out in 1926 from Clapham to Morden, the Piccadilly line from Finsbury to Cockfosters and westwards from Hammersmith to Hounslow. In 1925 the original tube line, the Metropolitan, which had first combined steam and electric trains, was electrified as far as Rickmansworth. The area around Harrow and Rickmansworth became known as Metroland where builders with sufficient foresight to buy up land made fortunes selling houses.

Dormitory suburbs grew up wherever the tube lines stretched. Morden was typical: its population grew in a few years by 25,000. In 1926 the *Daily Express* asked "What will London be like in 1930? How soon will the population reach the ten million mark?" The growth and shape of all towns in the inter-war years was governed by changing transport patterns. London spread outwards above its thrusting tube tunnels; along the extensions of the electrified Southern Railway on its way to Brighton, Hastings and Portsmouth, and along its bus routes. Towns like Leeds and Birmingham swelled after the introduction of motor buses.

Suburbs

People working in the town centres did not want to live in tenement flats in the smoky industrial areas. Buses enabled them to indulge their preference for a detached or semi-detached house with a small garden. If not on a new estate (see Chapter 6) the house was probably one of a long line strung along the main roads radiating out of the town. The practice of building in this way instead of in neighbourly clusters came to be known as ribbon development. In the mid-twenties it became obligatory to provide service roads to prevent driveways opening directly onto the lines of through traffic. At intervals along the now residential main roads, lines of houses would branch off at right angles down side roads which petered out into green fields. Gradually subsidiary roads opened off them and the suburb was born.

Motor traffic on the Great West Road. Houses were built along the main roads out of the towns.

The pull of the main roads was strong. Like the semi-detached houses, the shopping area of each suburb tended to keep to them. Housewives had to contend with increasing numbers of lorries lumbering along the arterial road which was also their local shopping street. Houses and shops were punctuated by petrol stations to serve the through traffic. Before 1920 petrol was generally obtained from cans, not pumps. In that year the Automobile Association opened the first garage with hand pumps at Aldermaston in Berkshire. They then appeared like an ugly rash at intervals on all main roads across the country.

Roads

No attempt was made to plan or control the ugliness of the new petrol stations or the ribbon development of suburban semis along arterial roads. In London the government had intervened successfully to create a sponsored monopoly of public transport under the Passenger Transport Board. The metropolitan underground system was one of the best organised in the world. Such planning did not extend to the country's road system. In most English minds large-scale road schemes were associated with dictatorship: Hitler and Mussolini were the road-makers

This advertisement of 1936 reflects contemporary concern about the ugliness of "ribbon development."

BANISH RIBBON DEVELOPMENT!
Write for illustrated booklet "Concrete Roads" sent free on request to the Cement and Concrete Association, Dept. AD-2, 52 Grosvenor Gardens, London, S.W.1.

HERE landscape gardening is called in, to add beauty to the incomparable safety of a concrete road. Velvety lawns, instead of unkempt grass verges, border the highway. Trees and flowering shrubs give travellers the illusion of passing through mile after mile of beautiful parkland.

Banish ribbon development! Our arterial roads should have beauty as well as utility. The enormous saving in upkeep when a concrete surface is used, would amply defray the cost of keeping lawns and borders in order, and surely it would be better for some of our unemployed to earn money in this way instead of drawing the Dole?

Concrete is the key to so many road improvements. Concrete needs no expensive "dressings"—it is always non-skid. Instead of deteriorating it gets stronger with age. That is why its upkeep costs are negligible, and the savings so effected can be applied to finance such improvements as this, and road safety necessities such as "Under and over" crossings, level crossing ramps, cyclist paths and school children subway crossings.

As cars increased in number so did petrol stations. This is a very early station, photographed in 1921.

of the inter-war years. It was, moreover, easier in a dictatorship than a democracy to provide the money and acquire the private property necessary for new roads. Lloyd George unsuccessfully advocated an ambitious road building scheme; the second Labour government refused to accept Oswald Mosley's demand for vast road works. It was not only that MacDonald and Philip Snowden, Chancellor of the Exchequer, were sceptical about the number of jobs such a scheme would engender: the Ministry of Transport underestimated traffic needs. It also refused to recommend 100 per cent grants for road building to local authorities, arguing that they must be responsible for their own amenities.

However, some new roads were built: from Perth to Inverness, from Edinburgh to Glasgow and from Liverpool to the towns of East Lancashire. The road tunnel under the Mersey connecting Liverpool and Birkenhead was completed in 1928. In the same year two vital bridges on the Great North Road were built over the Tyne at Newcastle and over the Tweed at Berwick. The North Circular Road and the Kingston Bypass—opened in 1927—the Watford Bypass and the Great West Road relieved pressure on the roads out of London. The routes to Dover, Brighton and Southend were improved. Further improvements came after 1936 when inter-city roads were taken over by the Ministry of Transport under the Trunk Road Act. Emphasis was put on maintenance and widening rather than new construction.

Lorries and delivery vans crowded the inter-city roads. Business firms maintained fleets of vans for distributing their own products. Many demobbed soldiers had bought up service vehicles at cheap rates and set up as road hauliers; they carried the goods which used to travel by rail. Even the milk churns were now picked up by lorries at the farm gate instead of being driven by the farmer to his nearest branch line station. The licensing of goods vehicles did not, as was expected, send produce back to the railways. The revolution in transport was apparent during the General Strike: if the vital arteries of the country had been the railways instead of the roads the outcome might well have been different.

Top. A milk train at
Paddington, 1928. Increasingly
after the war goods were being
sent by road. Post-war trains
were no faster than pre-war
until 1935 when the *Silver
Jubilee* (shown on right)
averaged 70 m.p.h. from
King's Cross to Newcastle.
But despite the faster trains
motor coach services attracted
passengers away from rail
travel. *Below right* Paddington
Station, 1932.

Railways

Britain's railways, taken over by the government in 1914, had received little maintenance during the war. They were worn out by 1918. Plans for their reconstruction and electrification were abandoned during the slump of 1921, falling victim to Geddes' Axe. The railways were handed back to private ownership like the coal mines. Under the Railways Act of 1921 the 120 existing small lines were grouped into four regions: the London Midland and Scottish (L.M.S.), the London and North Eastern (L.N.E.R.), the Great Western (G.W.R.) and the Southern Railway. Each group introduced new engine designs. The L.N.E.R. *Pacific*, the G.W.R. *Castle* and *King* pulled efficient expresses but were no faster than the pre-war trains. The breakthrough in speed came in the later thirties. In 1935 the L.N.E.R. *Silver Jubilee* travelled from Kings Cross to Newcastle at 70 m.p.h.; two years later the *Coronation* reached an average of 71 m.p.h. on its journey from Kings Cross to Edinburgh. But by then it was too late to restore the popularity of the railways. In 1928 the government had attempted to subsidise the industry by relieving it of three-quarters of its rates. The Southern Railway had been electrified in the thirties in order to attract passengers. But the railways went on losing money and were never able to lower fares as had been anticipated in the Railways Act. Passenger services were withdrawn from many branch lines: between 1930 and 1933 900 miles of line were closed down.

Goods were sent by lorry instead of train and passengers went by charabanc or motor coach. Originally the "sharrabang" or "sharra" was open to the skies and used for sightseeing trips. When it became a coach with a roof it travelled long distances, rivalling the railway in cost and convenience. Its great advantage was that it could be boarded in the suburbs instead of only at central—and dirty—stations. In 1921 a regular service started between London and Bristol. It was soon followed by services from the capital to Liverpool and Edinburgh and between most large towns under one hundred miles apart. Particularly popular were the coach routes from London to the south coast and to the seaside towns of East Anglia.

Effect of Transport on Country Life

Cities were now linked by coaches rushing along the arterial roads; rural towns and villages by smaller, slower local buses. Often the village carrier who had transported local produce and parcels in his horse-driven cart set up in business with one single-decker, acting as his own driver and conductor. Gradually the smaller men were bought up by larger companies.

Villagers who had lived very isolated lives could now travel by bus into the nearest market town to visit the library, the cinema, shops and friends. Moreover, the village shop could be supplied with more varied and fresher goods. Children could travel to the larger secondary schools in the towns instead of staying at the tiny village school; their fathers could go to work in shops and factories. Gradually they left their less lucrative village trades such as thatching and baking. Blacksmiths disappeared as the car superseded the horse.

The development of the motor bus enabled more people to get into the country (below).

BURNHAM BEECHES
BY MOTOR BUS

"Charabanc" trippers meet an obstacle in a country lane. Country roads remained much as they had been before the war.

Farmers' sons were often drawn to the new garages on the main roads instead of into the fields. They worked the petrol pumps while their sisters became waitresses in the roadside cafés catering for the increasing numbers of lorry drivers and motorists. The decline in farming as an occupation was due partly to the slump, partly to the motor engine: the bus enabled workers to get to the towns and the tractor made many of them redundant on the land. In spite of the National Government's subsidies and import restrictions and the setting up of marketing boards for bacon, potatoes, hops and milk, the number of agricultural workers dropped by half. There were 711,000 in 1939 as opposed to 1,429,000 in 1914. Villages within twenty miles of market towns tended to become outlying suburbs. With easy access, it was often more profitable to develop land for housing than to farm it.

Buses and coaches provided a two-way traffic. As well as taking villagers to their nearest towns they brought the townspeople into the countryside. Charabanc companies ran day excursions—often for school and club outings—to beauty spots. Like the inter-city services they took passengers away from the trains. In 1931 the Metropolitan Railway responded by introducing special excursions from London out to Rickmansworth, then still countryside, at less than cheap day fares. Other lines followed suit into the Home Counties. On Good Friday, 1932, the Great Western ran a special Hikers' Mystery Express to an unknown country destination. On a Saturday night in July the same year Southern Railways organised a moonlight walk over the South Downs to witness the sunrise from Chanctonbury Ring. So many people turned up that four trains had to be provided to carry them.

Walking

Paradoxically, motor transport encouraged the urban British to walk. The charabancs and cheap rail excursions disgorged the ramblers with their sensible shoes, berets, shorts or tweed skirts, and rucksacks. They explored the countryside for a day before returning to base and transport.

Opposite and below. Walking and cycling were popular leisure activities.

Soon a day was not sufficient to satisfy their sense of adventure. But it was very difficult to find reasonable accommodation for the night. J. B. Priestley complained in *John o'London's Weekly* in 1930 about "this searching for a bed at anything like a reasonable price, going round almost cap-in-hand when you ought to have been resting." The answer was the Youth Hostels Association. In 1930 Jack Catchpool raised the money to buy Pennant Hall in North Wales and the Old City Mill at Winchester and convert them into hostels. Membership of the Association cost 2s. 6d. (12½p.) a year and entitled card holders to a bed, supper at 1s. 6d. (7½p.) and breakfast at 1s. (5p.) so long as they arrived on foot or a bicycle. Bikes could be bought on the new hire-purchase system for 2s. (10p.) a week; cycling clubs proliferated during the thirties. Nine years after the founding of the Y.H.A., 83,418 hostellers were making use of 297 hostels.

Walking was not an expensive pastime. The popularity of rambling, hiking and climbing grew during the worst years of the Depression when there was not only a shortage of ready cash but time to spare. A leading Scottish mountaineer of the late thirties described recently on the radio how he took up the recreation when he and his unemployed neighbours started walking from Glasgow into the countryside: "We explored Loch Lomond and the Campsie Hills, and we started camping out. One night round the camp fire we decided to start a mountaineering club . . . I believe that during the slump there were many of the despairing and the disillusioned who found a new meaning to life in the countryside."

Nudism

Jack Catchpool had taken the idea of youth hostelling from Germany where fresh air had first become fashionable. The Germans had discovered that their children, undernourished during the war, benefitted enormously by exposure to sunlight. It followed that the direct rays of the sun were also good for healthy bodies. This theory, together with the current psychological belief that repressions would vanish once the human body could be taken for granted, led to the setting up of nudist societies. Perhaps two dozen were opened during the twenties; nearly all were in the South where the sun was expected to shine more often, in country houses near enough to suburban London to be accessible by car. Secretaries of the new societies were astonished at the initial response from middle aged as well as younger aspiring members. Applicants were only accepted if single or with the permission of spouse or fiancé. Nudism was attacked by the press but caused no great scandal. In fact the dankness of the climate and the monotony of camp routine soon put an end to the craze.

Holidays

Desire for the sun encouraged the wealthy to go south. The Cote d'Azur, Monte Carlo and the Venice Lido became fashionable for the few. Middle class people began to travel abroad to Scandinavia and Holland; and as the thirties progressed Mussolini and Hitler did not deter them

Blackpool, 1922 (opposite top) and Brighton, 1937 (opposite bottom). In the bottom picture, bathing machines have disappeared, amongst other things!

The changes in bathing dress from the early twenties (left) to 1937 (below).

A bank holiday scene. Apart from bank holidays only a small proportion of the working population could afford to take a week or two off every year.

from visiting Italy and Germany. The majority were lucky to have a holiday at all apart from the odd day's charabanc excursion to the country, the south coast or Blackpool. On August Bank Holiday 1937 half a million visitors arrived at Blackpool in 50,000 motor coaches and 700 trains. But only 1½ million workers in the twenties were entitled to a holiday with pay. Largely due to the efforts of the Amalgamated Engineering Union, this figure had been doubled by 1938. That year marchers in the May day rallies carried banners with the slogan

"Five days a week
Eight hours a day
Trade Union rates
And holidays with pay."

The Minister of Labour appointed a committee to examine the question. Its recommendation that a week's holiday with pay should be the general rule resulted in the Holidays with Pay Act (1938). Even this covered only half the working population; and only a third of workers earning under £4 a week could afford to go away for their holiday. Those who could pay for a break went to seaside boarding houses at resorts like Margate and Southend. At first they would buy their own food at the local shops and ask the landlady to cook it for them. By the early thirties she usually required them to pay for full board.

Boarding house holidays depended on the landlady's good nature, were relatively expensive and offered no entertainment for the family. The week, if wet, could be miserable. A young Canadian, Billy Butlin, running hoop-la stalls and bumper cars on fairgrounds, understood a need that had already been filled in his own country. He saved enough over fifteen years to buy a sixty acre field in Skegness and built chalets for 15,000 people, together with a large dining room and ballroom, swimming pool, shops and playground. In a quarter-page advertisement early in 1936 he announced the first holiday camp for the family. A week would cost £4. To his delight, 10,000 replies arrived: Butlin holiday camps were in business. Another, at Clacton, opened in 1937. Others, though none so successfully, followed Butlin's example. By 1939 holiday camps provided accommodation for half a million people.

Flying

Billy Butlin had persuaded Amy Johnson to open his holiday camp at Skegness. The publicity was excellent. In 1930 the girl from Hull who had saved up her £5 a week clerk's wages to take flying lessons had become a heroine: she flew alone from England to Australia. She received £10,000 from the *Daily Mail*, a C.B.E. from the King and the accolade of a Tin Pan Alley popular song:

"Amy, wonderful Amy
I'm proud of the way you flew
Believe me Amy, you cannot blame me
Amy, for falling in love with you."

The *Daily Mail* had made its original offer of a £10,000 prize in 1913

for the first crossing of the Atlantic in a heavier-than-air machine. Interest in flying was stimulated by the war. In 1918 the Royal Flying Corps became the Royal Air Force. Early the following year the British Air Ministry formed a Civil Department. A regular daily air service began between Hounslow and Paris. Only two or three passengers could be carried at a time; each paid £21 for the ride.

A month after the first civil flight to Paris the *Daily Mail* awarded its prize. In June a converted twin-engined bomber left St. Johns, Newfoundland. Aboard were pilot Captain John Alcock and navigator Lieutenant A. Whitten-Brown. They flew to Ireland in 16 hours 27 minutes at an average speed of 117 m.p.h., and received their £10,000 and a knighthood each. 1919 was a good year for record breaking. In November Ross and Keith Smith flew to Australia in 135 hours flying time, taking 28 days including stops. In their book *14,000 Miles through the Air* they explained how they had to economise on the weight they carried, leaving behind all personal kit: "For food we carried an emergency ration of tinned meat and biscuits. A fishing line and a few hooks were carried in case we should land on some uninhabited island and have to do the Robinson Crusoe act." Between 1924 and 1926 Alan Cobham made flights to Rangoon, Cape Town and Australia, bringing back valuable information about weather conditions, routes and landing grounds. Colonel Charles Lindbergh flew alone from New York to Paris in 1927. Another astonishing solo flight was made the following year by Bert Hinkler from London to Australia in fifteen days: four days faster and two years earlier than Amy Johnson.

Meanwhile civil flying was lagging behind the aviators. Cobham complained that when he returned from Africa "We simply couldn't wake the government up to the fact that we could start airlines all over the world. Nobody in Parliament seemed interested." Perhaps the commercial failure of the first cross-Channel flights in the face of French competition influenced the attitude of M.P.s. Government subsidies proved inadequate to prop up the private companies involved. In 1923 the Secretary of State for Air appointed a committee on civil aerial transport. Its report recommended the creation of a single company to replace the existing ones. Imperial Airways (ancestor of B.E.A. and B.O.A.C., now British Airways) was formed in 1924 and given a large subsidy. Daily services began to Paris, Cologne, Zurich and the Channel Islands and thrice

Alan Cobham arriving in London in 1926 after his record flight from Australia. He was a strong advocate of civil aviation.

An Imperial Airways' aeroplane at Croydon Airport. There was little demand for civil aviation during the period and not much encouragement from government.

weekly services to Amsterdam and Berlin. Three-engined planes were now used, carrying nineteen passengers and three crew. In the late twenties and early thirties regular services began to Genoa, Karachi, Delhi and Singapore.

There was no public demand for the expensive new method of travel. Internal services in Britain did not begin until 1930. In fact there was much opposition to the investment of public money on airways. In the preface to *The Great Delusion* (1927) written by Marion Acworth under the pseudonym "Neon," A. H. Pollen denied that aircraft were important either for transport in peace or for defence in war: "How are we to explain that an impoverished nation, crippled by debt, industrial disputes and unemployment can afford to spend over twenty millions a year on an activity the proved practical value of which is very small?"

Most of the twenty millions were used by the government to develop the giant airships. In 1916 a German Zeppelin had been shot down near Colchester. Its design was used by the R.A.F. for its own airships. The R34 was, at 643 feet, as long as an ocean liner and travelled at 60 m.p.h. In 1919 she crossed the Atlantic in both directions. Her crew were congratulated by the King but themselves felt doubtful about the usefulness of their airship, pointing out that moisture had been absorbed during the flight, weighing the aircraft down. Their fears were justified: in 1921 R34 was wrecked and R38 crashed in trials over the Humber, killing forty-four passengers. In spite of the equally catastrophic experiences of French and American airships, the National Government persevered. On 4th May, 1924, Ramsay MacDonald told the House of Commons that "It is essential to carry into effect a constructive programme of airship development." Work began on the R100 and R101. In November, 1926, the *Daily Telegraph* reported: "The accommodation will include sleeping cabins with two or four berths, promenade decks, lounges and smoking rooms; the dining rooms will be capable of seating 50 people at a time." On 5th October, 1930, the R101 set out on its maiden voyage to India. On board were 48 crew and six passengers, including Lord Thomson, Secretary of State for Air and personal friend of MacDonald. Over Beauvais in Northern France it ran into a squall and came down in flames. Only six of the crew survived. A week later half a million people watched the funeral procession of the victims as it wound its way through London.

Strangely enough, the R101 crash was followed by a surge of enlistment into the R.A.F. Maybe rising unemployment was the cause. The failure of this method of crossing the Atlantic and the demand for jobs both encouraged the government to grant subsidies to Cunard for the building of the *Queen Mary*. In any case, the tragedy was the end not only of the R101 but of all British airships. The government now turned its attention to extending civil aviation to India, Africa and Australia. To the majority of their electors, of course, such activities were quite uninteresting. The aeroplane may have been the new wonder of the age and the solo fliers the new heroes; but it affected British people far less than the motor car and the motor bus which changed the shape of towns and villages as well as the everyday life of their inhabitants.

The R101 airship before and after it crashed.

6 Home and Health

Housing Shortage

SIX HUNDRED THOUSAND families in Britain needed homes when the armistice was signed. A local authority housing manager told Charles Masterman: "There are about 500 applications on the books. Some have been seeking houses for three years without success. One of these begged me today to get his case considered. He and his wife and four children are living in two small rooms in a six room cottage. Two other families occupy the remaining four rooms." Even if all building had not been stopped during the war, the growing population would have caused a housing shortage. Moreover, four years' lack of proper maintenance meant that more property than usual was becoming derelict each year.

In 1915 existing rents had been frozen by the Rent and Mortgage Restriction Act. This was just part of the wartime machinery to control the prices of necessities. But its significance outlasted the war. The government had taken responsibility for housing for the first time; it could not suddenly give it up, especially at a time of great shortage. The demand created by the war years put up the price of houses and building costs rose dramatically just after the war because of the demand for higher wages. Economic rents were therefore far higher than the figures at which they had been frozen in 1915. What was the government to do? De-control would mean eviction for vast numbers of tenants unable to pay realistic rents.

Council Houses

Lloyd George's answer was the Housing Act of 1919. Responsibility for the supply of new housing was to be shouldered by the government. Christopher Addison's Act directed local authorities to provide as many houses as were needed in their areas and to send the bill for any expense not covered by the levy of a penny rate to the Treasury. The only condition imposed on this largesse was that plans had to be approved by the Ministry of Health. Private builders also received subsidies if they submitted plans. In the four years of the Act's life local authorities put up 170,000 and private builders 40,000 houses. 54,000 more were built privately without subsidy. Even so, these figures were not sufficient to meet the post-war demand. More important, the bills presented to the Treasury were enormous. No local authority was going to economise on its plans knowing it would not have to meet the cost. With the slump of

Opposite. Housing minister Christopher Addison lays the first concrete slab of a council house, 1920.

79

1921 the Act succumbed to Geddes' economies: Addison lost his job, local authorities their grants and private builders their subsidies.

Addison's lump subsidies were blamed for inflation. Instead, Neville Chamberlain's and Charles Wheatley's Acts of 1923 and 1924 granted small annual subsidies of £6 and £9 per house. Chamberlain encouraged the building of houses for sale; Wheatley put the onus back on local authorities to build houses to rent. Over two million houses were built under these schemes between 1923 and 1934. Independent builders put up three million more in the thirties. The boom in private building depended on the growth of the building societies: small down payments enabled more people to buy their own homes, the mortgage repayment being little more each month than a normal rent.

The new local authority houses provided the minimum of three bedrooms, living room, kitchen and bathroom demanded by ministry regulations in return for a subsidy. They were built on new municipal housing estates on the outskirts of towns, now accessible by public transport or private car. The estates varied in size: relatively small like the one at East Acton in West London, larger like Wythenshawe outside Manchester and Kingstanding on the outskirts of Birmingham (30,000 people by 1932); or enormous like Becontree near Dagenham in Essex. This was begun in 1921 by the London County Council and housed over 100,000 by 1932. Whatever their size, the estates looked much alike. The two-storied houses, mostly semi-detached but sometimes in groups of four or six, were built of brick often covered in rough-cast or stucco and set back from the geometrically planned streets. Each had its strip of back garden but trees took a long time to grow sufficiently to soften the long lines of brick or stucco. Nor did communal buildings like libraries, schools or church halls help to counteract the bleakness of the estates. They had no integral life of their own but were merely dormitories for industrial towns.

Becontree, an enormous council estate housing 100,000 people. Begun in 1921 it was completed ten years later.

Private Houses

There was one attempt, at Welwyn Garden City in the early twenties, to plan a new town with pleasant housing, its own communal life and supporting light industry. It failed because only an engineering firm and the Shredded Wheat Company were induced to put up factories there. Welwyn became just another—albeit very attractive—dormitory suburb. Most private houses were built in long ribbon developments along the main roads (see Chapter 5). It was far cheaper to provide services like water and electricity if building followed existing pipe lines. Basically these houses were similar to the council houses but usually had two living rooms: it was the age of the "three up, two down." Some showed their superiority by mock Tudor timbers, leaded windows and irrelevant gables. Typical advertisements appearing in the press in the early thirties offered "attractive and well designed houses of quality . . . one minute to buses" with "English oak half-timbering." Prices for a three bedroomed house ranged from £450 in the provinces to £1,450 in London. The most luxurious offered panelled "lounge halls" instead of the usual narrow corridor leading from the front door to the kitchen at the back.

Movement from Town Centres

The new estates and suburbs were quickly filled; the population was not only badly housed but on the move. Workers left the textile and ship-building towns of the North to find work in the new factories at Coventry, Birmingham and Luton. The towns in the South-East and West of England spread into their suburbs, increasing at the expense of those in the North and in South Wales. In the twenties the population of Wales declined by 3 per cent and of Scotland by 0·8 per cent. In both North and South there was movement away from the town centres. Few chose to live in them any more. The aristocracy, like the Duke of Westminster who sold Grosvenor House in London to be knocked down and replaced by a hotel in 1930, gave up their town residences in response to death duties. The middle class left the older parts of town for their more

Private house styles—*above*
1922; *right* c. 1930.

For those unable to afford private or council housing this was often the sort of environment in which they had to live. A scene in Tyneside.

comfortable suburban houses; the better-off workers moved from their urban Victorian terraces out to the council estates. But the weekly rent of council houses was too high for any worker earning less than the average wage of £4 a week; in one town, Birmingham, over three-quarters of all families had an income less than this as late as 1934.

The council estates created a new class barrier between the better-off workers and those who could not afford to pay their rents. Housing policy between the wars, in spite of Addison's and Wheatley's Acts, failed to provide sufficient homes for the lower-paid workers, let alone the unemployed. It was these two groups who were left with their families in the rapidly deteriorating Victorian and Edwardian terraces or back-to-backs in the town centres. There were no bathrooms in the dark narrow houses, no hot water and only an outside lavatory. The semis on the council estates might be criticised on aesthetic grounds but they did have plumbing and electricity. In the urban terrace houses all washing was done at the kitchen sink under the cold tap except on Saturdays, when water was boiled on the kitchen range for the weekly bath in a zinc tub. The terraces were built too close to those opposite to allow any sunlight into their windows which were in any case grimy from the smoke of nearby factories. Instead of gardens they had, as Rowntree described, "asphalted backyards opening on to narrow back lanes used for the removal of house refuse and for carting coal. A few of these are only four feet wide. The streets are drab, dull and unlovely."

Conditions varied over the country. Housing in the poorer areas deteriorated. Once Addison's Act had been jettisoned council authorities in districts like South Wales or the North-East had no incentive to build: even with the annual subsidy they had no hope of building houses their workers could afford to rent. The areas needing most help in the form of subsidies therefore received none at all. In Edinburgh and Glasgow, where home for most families was one or two rooms in a tenement house, new building lagged far behind the demands of the growing population. Overcrowded tenements and Victorian terraces rapidly deteriorated into slums.

Inside a tenement slum in
Bethnal Green, East London
in 1923.

Slums

Before the war campaigns for the abolition of slums had been left to local
reformers and individual groups. When the government took over responsibility for housing in 1919 it concentrated on building new houses.
Very little slum clearance took place during the twenties; only 17,000
were rehoused. Arthur Greenwood, Minister of Health in the second
Labour government, gave the task to local authorities under his 1930
Housing Act. Their incentive was a subsidy dependent on the number of
families rehoused and the cost of rehousing them. But the 1931 economic
crisis wrecked their five-year plans for clearing the slums. In 1933 there
were a million homes in England and Wales considered unfit to be lived
in, 60,000 more in Scotland. In Manchester alone there were 30,000.
Over 51,000 houses in Birmingham could not boast a lavatory, inside or
out. In York in 1935 Rowntree found a typical back-to-back house:
"Portions of the external walls have perished. The roof is sagging. The
W.C. is shared by two families. The floor of the living room is of brick and
is broken and damp. The fire-place is broken. The plaster on the walls
and ceiling is loose and the walls are damp. Coals are kept in a cupboard
under the stairs. There is no hand rail on the staircase."

By 1938 only half the country's slums had been cleared; over 200,000
families still made their homes in so-called uninhabitable houses. It was
considered an achievement in York that only 11 per cent of the working

Of Sheffield (left) George Orwell wrote: "If at rare moments you stop smelling sulphur it is because you have begun smelling gas." Such pollution was typical of industrial towns.

population lived in slum conditions in 1936 as opposed to 26 per cent in 1900. On the other hand, overcrowding was reduced by the movement of the lowest paid into the less dilapidated terrace houses vacated by the new council house tenants. And the general standard of housing, notwithstanding the slums, was far higher in 1939 than it had been in 1919: at least the majority of houses now boasted their own water supplies and lavatories.

It was not easy to bring up a healthy family in damp, dark houses with no running water, a communal lavatory and bedrooms—if not beds—shared by adults as well as children. In such conditions tuberculosis, pneumonia and bronchitis flourished. Between 1922 and 1924 T.B. killed 1,066 people out of every million of the population. By 1937, with improved housing conditions, its victims had dropped to 657. The figure remained higher in Durham, South Wales and other areas where there was little slum clearance or new building and much unemployment. In York the disease accounted for 73 per cent of all deaths in 1935.

Health Gradually Improves

Improved hospitals as well as better housing were needed to fight the old diseases. The standard of both medical attention and conditions in the wards was low. In her book *Give it Time: an experience of hospitals, 1928–32,* published in 1974, Bella Aranovitch recalled how she had been shunted from bed to bed in voluntary and public hospitals in the East End of London while the painful suppurating wound resulting from her appendix operation was virtually ignored by doctors for five years. In the enormous wards the beds were tightly packed in four rows so that the inner rows were far from the light of the window; patients were known by numbers instead of their names, left with their hair unwashed and only allowed visitors twice a week.

In 1935 a third of the country's 3,029 hospitals were still run by voluntary organisations. But an increasing number of public hospitals were gradually providing better treatment for more people. In 1936 national health insurance covered half the population, although it did not extend either to dependents or to the self-employed. Probably even more important was the gradual acceptance of a higher standard of hygiene, a balanced diet and fresh air. The vogue for the latter was taken up by the medical profession as well as the hikers and nudists. When a doctor published a handbook in 1934 entitled *Useful Knowledge for Health and Home* he thought it necessary to spell out that "Fresh air never caused illness; it is draughts that have to be avoided. It is of vital importance to

A London hospital. The flowers were given by Dutch bulb growers.

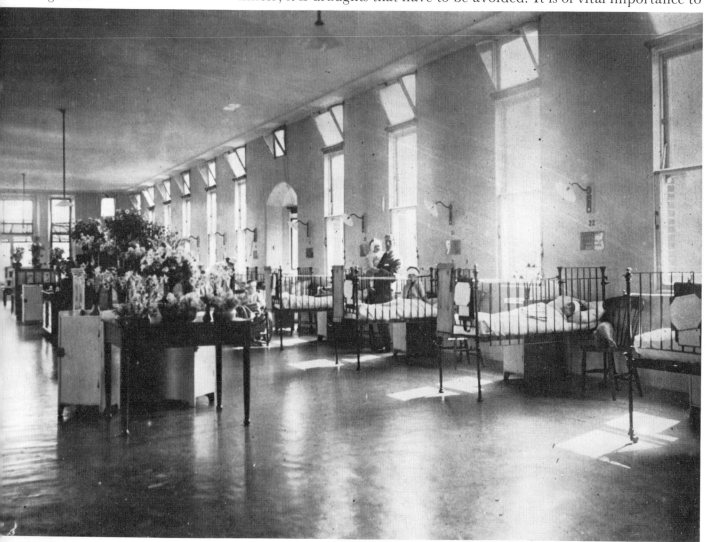

have ventilation; to continually breathe in a 'stuffy atmosphere' will produce headaches, drowsiness, lack of concentration and one's resistance is lowered and consequently influenza and other infectious diseases are the more easily contracted." In the towns the air was hardly fresh. George Orwell, in Sheffield, commented that "If at rare moments you stop smelling sulphur it is because you have begun smelling gas." It was not surprising that few people were in the habit of throwing open their windows. They were officially exhorted to take exercise as well as to breathe fresh air. A report by Sir John Boyd Orr for the Ministry of Agriculture in 1936 resulted the following year in the government's Physical Training Act. Grants were provided for the development of playing fields and recreation centres.

Middle class social workers were astonished at the attitudes of working women. Ignorance was not confined to the benefits of air and sunlight. These wives and mothers not only found it difficult to afford fruit and vegetables for their families; they had no idea such food would be better for them than their usual diet of bread and jam, fish and chips and tea. Boyd Orr's report showed that although consumption of nutritious food had increased since the end of the war, half the nation was living on an inadequate diet. Moreover, 20 per cent of all children had a very poor diet indeed. Nor were they particularly clean. The percentage of school children with lice or vermin in their hair dropped from 39·5 in 1912 to 7·9 in 1937; but country people were still horrified at the lack of basic hygiene, undernourished limbs and the unfamiliarity with running water displayed by evacuees from the slums who were billeted on them in 1939. Orwell, too, was shocked by the unhealthy appearance of Londoners. Caught in a crowd in Trafalgar Square, "It was impossible, looking about one then, not to be struck by the physical degeneracy of modern England. The people surrounding me were not working class people for the most part; they were the shopkeeper–commercial traveller type, with a sprinkling of the well-to-do. But what a set they looked! Puny limbs, sickly faces. . . . Hardly a well-built man or a decent looking woman, and not a fresh complexion anywhere."

However, the nation's health was gradually improving, as the decline in the infant mortality rate showed. Of every thousand babies born alive in England and Wales in 1913, 110 died before they were a year old. By 1925 the figure had dropped to 76. Ten years later it was 62 and in the late thirties 58. This was an average figure hiding regional differences. There was a direct relation between poverty and infant mortality: in Surrey the rate was 41, in Jarrow 114; in York there was a difference even within the working class. Rowntree found that 41 out of every thousand babies born to better-off families died as opposed to 77 born in the slums.

As fewer babies died and fewer young people succumbed to tuberculosis and bronchitis, the population grew. People over 65 made up 5 per cent of the population in 1921, 7 per cent in 1931. Emigration also decreased; indeed in the thirties immigrants outnumbered those leaving the country. There were over 42½ million people living in Great Britain in 1921. By 1939 there were 46½ million, in spite of a falling birth rate. As might be expected after a war, there was a rise in the rate in 1920; but after that fewer babies were born each year until the late thirties.

Graph showing births per thousand of the population.

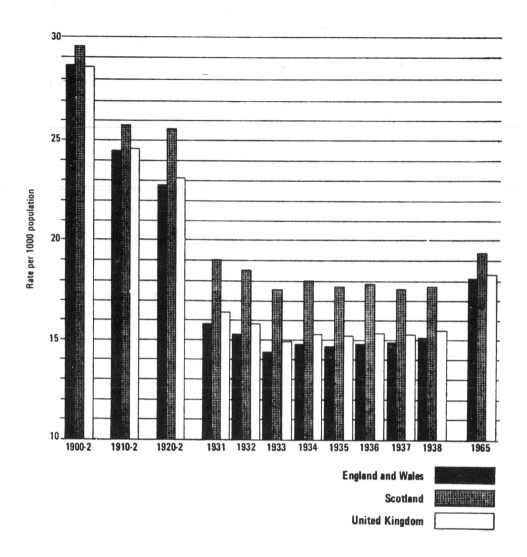

England and Wales ████
Scotland ▓▓▓▓
United Kingdom ☐

Fall in Birth Rate

Why did the birth rate fall? Statistics do not bear out the theory that later marriages were responsible. Nor did birth control by contraception have much to do with the change. Marie Stopes tried to publicise methods of contraception. Her book *Married Love*, her public meetings at the Queen's Hall, London, in 1922, her lectures around the country and her clinic in the Holloway Road all at first met with ridicule. Techniques of birth control were not even taught in the medical schools until after 1945. Before the war only the better off and the enlightened could obtain advice from private specialists. For the majority of women sex meant unwanted pregnancies. No wonder the abortion rate was high. Every chemist sold "silver coated quinine pills" for 7s. 6d. (37½p.) for 50, and newspapers carried advertisements for "Dr Reynold's lightening pills." Midwives gave evidence to the Birkett Committee in 1937 about the high incidence of backstreet and self-induced abortions. A *Lancet* editorial of the previous year commented that "in this country 16 to 20 per cent of all pregnancies are believed to terminate in abortion."

Economic considerations were probably most influential in bringing down the number of births. Charles Masterman wrote in 1922 of the effect of "high prices and cruel taxation:" "Everyone realises that as the desire for content and comfort is gradually sweeping away all questions of duty to the race or supernatural sanctions, it will find its expression more and more in the absence of marriage or in marriage without children. More babies means, literally, an injury to the babies already born; a worse education, smaller accommodation, less opportunity, scantier food." If the choice was between an additional baby in the nursery or a baby Austin in the garage, the car tended to win. Nor was the growing demand for a higher standard of living confined to the middle class. The strikes of 1921 indicated not only the stress of inflation but the belief of the working man after the war that he deserved a bigger share of the country's wealth. In 1933 the birth rate fell below 15 per 1,000, encouraging letters to the medical journals such as one warning that "the unchecked development of this attack on the strength of our race threatens the destruction of our ideals and our Empire."

Modern Conveniences

Other everyday comforts besides the car were becoming available to tempt the middle and better-off working classes. The new light industries

Manufacturing refrigerators, 1932.

Compared with pre-war houses, interiors in the twenties and thirties were simpler, lighter and less cluttered.

turned out vacuum cleaners, hair dryers and refrigerators. All could be bought on the new hire purchase system; all were dependent on the supply of electricity. The Central Electricity Board was set up in 1926 to centralise local generating stations and to bring cheaper power to British industry. It also speeded up the spread of electricity into the home, though speed was hardly the word if home was the countryside. Villagers and farmers saw pylons being built across the fields but only 3 per cent of farms were wired by 1929 and 60 per cent of rural houses still used oil lamps in 1939. By this time most people living in towns boasted electricity; it was one of the amenities offered by both the new council estates and private developments.

Labour-saving electrical equipment in the home became more popular as fewer housewives could afford servants. The same reason induced middle class families to leave their large Edwardian and Victorian houses. Their new semi-detached homes had fewer stairs to run up and down and keep clean, no attics for servants to sleep in. Instead of a dark basement scullery for the cook there was a bright tiled kitchen for the housewife equipped with electrical gadgets and a convenient hatch to the dining room. The rest of the house was smaller, simpler and less cluttered than the old Edwardian family establishment. It was also much lighter: at night, because of electric lighting; during the day because the new metal

Contemporary factory architecture.

window frames enabled larger expanses of glass to be used and because pale cream or yellow paints and distempers took the place of dark wallpapers. Fire grates in need of blacking surmounted by ornately carved dust-catching mantlepieces gave way to clinically tiled fireplaces. Often the heat came not from coal but from portable electric fires standing in the grate. Ornaments and photographs disappeared, as did the many small Victorian tables and large piano which used to hold them. Instead, the living room furniture usually comprised the three piece suite covered in pale rough moquette or a bright geometrical pattern, a large "pouffe" to serve as footstool or extra seat and a neat "nest" of tables. In the thirties bulky cocktail cabinets and tubular steel chairs appeared in middle class homes.

Architecture

Uncluttered clean lines made less headway outside houses than inside. The influence of the continental "modern architecture" could be seen in a few private houses by Maxwell Fry, the Highpoint flats at Highgate, London by the Russian architect Berthold Lubetkin, the Shakespeare Memorial Theatre at Stratford, the glass and steel *Daily Express* building in Fleet Street and some underground stations. But the modern movement forwarded by the *Architectural Review* never permeated mass housing. When the architect Walter Gropius escaped to London from Hitler's Germany where he had instigated the Bauhaus movement, he was horrified to find that most Englishmen preferred their home to be at best a neo-Georgian mini-mansion, like those designed by Lutyens for the newer part of Hampstead Garden Suburb, and at worst a semi-detached covered with mock Tudor timbers and ornate gables.

The *Daily Express* building (on right), Fleet Street, London.

Apart from the incidental theatre, block of flats or small housing development, the most contemporary looking buildings were the new factories lining the arterial roads. Pylons brought them electricity and lorries raw materials; they no longer had to be built near the coal mines of the North. Many are still visible, if somewhat dingier than in the thirties, along the Great West and North Circular roads in London and along many other roads on the outskirts of other large towns. Orwell described them in *The Road to Wigan Pier*: "The typical post-war factory is not a gaunt barrack or an awful chaos of blackness and belching chimneys; it is a glittering white structure of concrete, glass and steel, surrounded by green lawns and beds of tulips."

Mass-Produced Goods

The new factories produced gears and spare parts for cars, glassware,
radios, electrical equipment of all kinds and also packaged foodstuffs like
cereals, crisps, jellies and cake mixes. Branded and prepared goods made
both shopping and cooking easier for the housewife, especially as they
came wrapped in cellophane or in cardboard boxes. Soon butter, sugar
and biscuits would no longer be weighed out on the counter scales. Moreover, the goods were often now sold in the cheaper, more hygienic
multiple stores proliferating in the High Streets. Most suburbs and small
towns as well as big cities had their Macfisheries and their International
Stores. Seebohm Rowntree noted that in York in 1936 the small shopkeepers were losing their trade not only through the removal of the
resident population by slum clearance but also "through the competition
of chain stores and other low-priced shops in the city."

Rowntree also commented that stores like Woolworths, Marks and
Spencers and British Home Stores were providing a large range of goods
for people of limited means. For it was not only food but household goods
and clothes which were being mass produced in the factories. During the
war special chemicals had been used in aeroplane construction to make
the fabric covering the wooden framework taut and waterproof. When
peace brought cuts in the aircraft industry this chemical was used to
make rayon. Synthetic fibres revolutionised women's clothes. They were
cheaper and easier to make up in quantity than wool or cotton, lighter to
wear and simpler to launder. Underwear was less bulky than the old
cotton petticoats, stockings flesh coloured and light in weight instead of
dark and woollen.

Women's Opportunities

Changes in dress after the war were thus partly due to innovations in the chemical engineering industry. Also important was the changing position of women in society. Economic equality with men was still a dream (see Chapter 1), as indeed it still is. There was no question of equal pay for equal work: in shops, factories, the civil service and teaching men received larger pay packets for identical work. Opportunities for women to make successful careers for themselves were few but gradually increasing. Boards of large companies, university common rooms and the judicial bench were all male preserves, though the bar accepted Miss Lucy Williams in 1922. Viscountess Astor became the first woman M.P. in 1919 but was not followed by many others. Oxford University allowed women to take degrees in 1920, Cambridge not until 1948.

Nevertheless, their experience in the factories and on the land during the war had equipped girls for jobs in the new light industries, catering and expanding local government. At least the working class girl had an alternative to domestic service. The middle class girl could just about consider a career as an alternative to marriage, though she could not combine the two if she was a teacher or civil servant.

Fashions

Working girls needed clothes suited to their new life in the factory or multiple store; middle class housewives could not handle the hoover in the same corsets and long skirts in which they had given orders to those very factory workers and shop girls who used to be their servants. Women working with men seemed at first to want to ape their fashions. Brassieres came in but were designed to flatten the breasts. Waists were low. As skirts revealed more and more leg so hair was cut to reveal the ears. First it was bobbed, then shingled then almost disappeared in the Eton crop. A popular song of 1924 revealed the agonies of decision suffered by girls:

Women's fashion in 1926.

> "Sweet Susie Simpson had such lovely hair,
> It reached down to her waist;
> Till friends sweetly told her that around Mayfair
> Having hair was thought bad taste.
> 'Bobbed or shingled it must be dear',
> Said they, 'If you wish to wed;'
> Till in blank despair, in the fatal chair,
> At the hairdressers' shop she said:
> 'Shall I have it bobbed or shingled?
> Shall I have it shingled or bobbed?'
> Sister Cissie says 'Oh have it shorn short, Sue,
> Shingled shorn and shaven like the swell set do.'
> 'Shall I have it shingled shorter?'
> Said Sue as she sighed and sobbed;
> 'Sister Cissie says she'd sooner see it short and shingled,
> But both my brothers Bert and Bobbie say it's better bobbed.'"

The hard look created by shingled hair was emphasised by bright lip-

A dress of 1935.

stick, pale powder, rouge and nail varnish. In Macdonell's *England, their England* the neice of Lady Ormerode "had ivory coloured cheeks, orange lips, thin blackened eyebrows, close cut hair, pale pink ears and purple finger nails. She smoked all through dinner." Smoking was on the increase. In the evenings men puffed away at their cigars, women at their cigarettes, often held in long holders of jade or amber or their less expensive copies. Soldiers had learnt to smoke cigarettes in the trenches, women in the factory canteens. Now the habit was accepted in public places like the cinema and on tops of buses. Lloyd George, Prime Minister from 1918 to 1922, even lifted the ban on smoking at Cabinet meetings.

By the end of the twenties fashions were becoming less exaggerated. Perhaps the Depression brought restraint; perhaps skirts became longer because it was thought they should go up no further. Hair, like skirts, was lengthening again. Cigarettes were smoked less ostentatiously. A women's magazine referred in 1929 to "fashion's new discovery that the feminine figure is lovely." A new word, "uplift," entered the vocabulary. Jerseys, like the new style brassieres, emphasised female curves. Men, too, wore sweaters and pullovers on casual or sporty occasions for the first time. At a golf club described by Macdonell "there were purple jumpers and green jumpers and tartan jumpers; there were the biggest, the baggiest, the brightest plus fours that ever dulled the lustre of a peacock's tail." Men also adopted brighter ties, lighter suits, softer hats, wider trousers known as Oxford bags and suede shoes. Except in the city and civil service they even wore coloured shirts with soft collars to work.

Department stores and mass production meant that clerks could dress like bank managers and shop girls like society hostesses. But the new fashions did not hide all class differences—indeed, they seemed to strengthen them. The woman whose husband was unemployed or earned less than the average worker's £4 a week could not buy herself new clothes. She wore shapeless old skirts and aprons of sacking. Together with the strain caused by continual fear of pregnancy, a poor diet and inadequate housing, they made her look old and haggard before she was thirty.

The new fashions did make those women who could afford them feel more comfortable; but they were hardly the shocking liberating influence suggested by some myths about the "roaring twenties." In some ways they were surprisingly modest. Bathing costumes still had short sleeves and legs half way down the thigh; only in the thirties did the daring low back come in. Contemporary moralists suspected that painted finger nails and lips, short hair and skirts and long cigarette holders implied sexual promiscuity. But then they also considered immoral John van Druten's harmless play *Young Woodley* about a schoolboy falling in love with his housemaster's wife, and Radclyffe Hall's *The Well of Loneliness*, a mild and romanticised account of lesbian life. Both the play and the book were banned, as was Marie Stopes' *Married Love*.

Morality

Divorce was frowned upon as much as birth control. And, like contraception, it was only available to the better off and to those who knew where to find the necessary lawyer or specialist. The divorce rate increased. There were under 1,000 divorces in 1913, over 4,500 in 1928 and over 7,000 in 1938. The increase at the end of the thirties was due to A. P. Herbert's private Bill which became the 1937 Divorce Act and made desertion and insanity as well as adultery grounds for divorce after three years.

The morality of the twenties has been judged by contemporary reactions to birth control, divorce and censorship and also by the heroines of novels by D. H. Lawrence and Aldous Huxley. But Lucy Tantamount in Huxley's *Point, Counter Point* was hardly typical of the average girl in Britain between the wars. The latter was jolly rather than promiscuous. She was to some extent liberated by her clothes and her easily-run home; and she could now travel alone on public transport. However, she had nothing like equality of opportunity with her brothers. And if she was unfortunate enough to be the daughter or wife of a low paid or unemployed worker she couldn't even afford the outward signs of liberation, the new fashions or the lipstick. If she took a job the means test might deprive the head of the household of his insurance benefit. There was no freedom for the working class woman in the slums.

THE THREAT
of losing a trim slender figure

HOW TO
AVOID THAT
FUTURE SHADOW

Ask your doctor! Over-weight is harmful. It makes for sluggish health and destroys the trim, slender figure of fashion. And over-weight is generally caused by eating between meals. So don't eat between meals. That's the time to **smoke a Kensitas instead.** Your desire will be pleasantly forgotten in the mellow satisfaction of the appetising aroma of Kensitas. Don't eat between meals, **smoke a Kensitas instead.**

, good as really good cigarettes can be

"Your Kensitas arettes Sir"

MANUFACTURED BY THE
KENSITAS
PRIVATE
PROCESS

In the early twenties smoking by women was frowned upon. But, as this advertisement of 1929 shows, attitudes to smoking had changed as the decade went on.

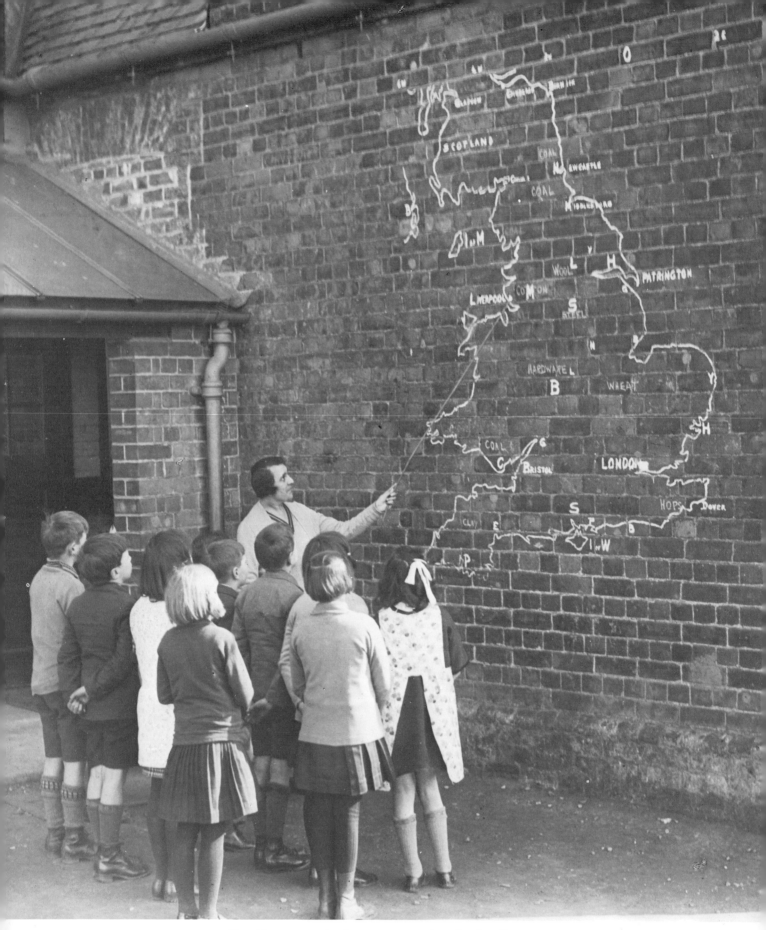

Teaching geography from a map on the school wall, 1930.

7 School

Education and Social Class

IN 1918 the education of every child depended upon the status of his family. If his father was a member of the upper class he went to an expensive private boarding school until he was thirteen, then to one of the public schools. Should he be heir to a title, that public school would undoubtedly be Eton or Harrow. If his father came from the professional middle class he would probably go to a grammar school at 11 and stay until 16 or 18. If he came from a working class family he would go to an elementary school; if particularly intelligent he might win a scholarship to grammar school. But if he was only moderately bright or if his parents had no wish to see him well educated he would leave his elementary school at fourteen at the latest. Forty per cent of British children in 1918 left school before they reached this age. Many only attended school part-time. This was because the old Factory Acts had allowed children to be educated three days a week and employed in industry during the other three working days. The lower age limit for part-time schooling had been raised to twelve at the end of the nineteenth century but the practice lingered on. Before the war 70,000 12 and 13 year-olds were employed in agricultural work three days a week.

Plans for improvement and rationalisation had to be shelved during the 1914–18 war. The war itself brought further problems. Teachers were called up to fight; 743 schools were requisitioned for hospitals, training centres and refugee camps. Children had to be taught by unqualified teachers in enormous classes in church and public halls. As accommodation had to be shared, many only attended part-time.

Fisher's Act, 1918

Once the war was over there was a demand for better facilities. There was also a demand for more secondary education: the many trained men killed in the trenches had to be replaced. Munition workers and workers in other key industries were now better paid than they had ever been; many were both willing and able to pay the necessary £3 to £6 a term for secondary education for their children.

Lloyd George was sympathetic towards these demands. He decided that the policy of the Board of Education must be guided by the best brains and the most experienced educationists that could be found. He

H. A. L. Fisher, President of the Board of Education. His Act of 1918 introduced important changes in education.

therefore appointed H. A. L. Fisher, then Vice Chancellor of Sheffield University, as President of the Board. Fisher's Act of 1918 remedied the worst defects in the old system. No child could leave school until the last day of the term in which he had his fourteenth birthday. Nor was any part-time employment permitted; the only work available to a child was the early morning paper round. Local authorities were given grants to improve their school buildings. They were also encouraged to grant more scholarships to bright elementary school children so that they could go to secondary schools. There they were able to take the School Certificate and Higher School Certificate examinations. These had been introduced in 1917 and were now co-ordinated under the Board of Education.

Fisher realised the success of the new education system would depend upon the teachers. They had always been badly paid. Now they suffered from the rising cost of living. Assistant teachers earned a maximum of £160 a year; only £140 if they were women. Elementary school teachers earned anything between £70 and £120. Fisher appointed a committee under Lord Burnham to look into salaries. The new Burnham scale laid down the rate to be paid for each teaching post with bonuses for extra qualifications. Salaries for assistant teachers went up to £310 for men, £254 for women. All were eligible for national pensions. The profession began to attract people of higher calibre whose influence was soon felt in the schools. More important, the salary rate was standardised throughout the country. Previously the wealthier local authorities had offered higher rates of pay and the poorer areas had been unable to attract the better teachers.

The 1918 Act was not completely successful. Fisher's proposals for part-time education for adolescents up to 16 who had left school at 14 did not materialise. He wanted them to attend continuation schools one day a week. But neither local authorities nor employers were co-operative. After 1921 only Rugby made attendance compulsory. By 1938 the country could boast only 51,000 day release students.

Fisher was concerned with the child at every age: before he was five as well as during and after his schooldays. He gave local authorities the power to open nursery schools. But, as with continuation schools, they were voluntary powers. Only 114 nursery schools had been opened by 1939, not all of them by local authorities. It was left to individuals like Rachel and Margaret Macmillan to encourage their development. The sisters had held day camps for the children of working mothers during the war. Often they shocked local people by using churchyards. In 1923 they founded the Nursery Schools Association, setting up some schools and campaigning for others.

The "Eleven Plus"

Projected nursery and continuation schools, like additional buildings and free places and also teachers' salaries, were hit by the slump of 1921. But Geddes' economies were reversed when the Labour Party won office for the first time in 1924. C. P. Trevelyan, the new President of the Board of Education, commissioned R. H. Tawney the historian to draft a state-

A classroom scene in a boy's secondary school, 1922.

ment of Labour Party policy. Tawney wrote a paper entitled "Secondary Education for All": "The Labour Party is convinced that the only policy which is at once educationally sound and suited to a democratic community is one under which primary education and secondary education are organised as two stages in a single continuous process; its objective therefore is both the improvement of primary education and the development of public secondary education to such a point that all normal children, irrespective of the income, class or occupation of their parents, may be transferred at the age of 'eleven plus' from the primary or preparatory school and remain in the latter till sixteen." These proposals were put forward in a report drawn up by a committee of the Board under Sir Henry Hadow.

Trevelyan lost the battle for raising the school leaving age, even though the Hadow Report compromised at 15 instead of 16. But the recommendation for the break in schooling at 11 set the future pattern for public education. Some local authorities like London and Manchester had set up separate "central" or "modern" schools for selected children over eleven as early as 1911. All authorities were now directed to follow their example and reorganise their schools according to the Hadow Report. They did so slowly. Often there were difficulties where local authorities overlapped; church and other voluntary elementary schools were often less than eager to send their pupils at eleven to open state

schools. On the other hand reorganisation was helped by the ability of children to travel further afield to their new schools on the local buses. Just as the coming of the railways had enabled upper class parents in the nineteenth century to send their children away to public boarding schools, so now the motor bus encouraged the development of the secondary school. By 1939 two-thirds of the country's children left their elementary schools when they reached eleven and went to a grammar or a modern school.

Improved Schools

At the outbreak of the Second World War a deprived third of all children therefore still received all their education at their elementary school. Elementary schools were re-named primary schools after 1926. Some, especially in rural areas, remained in their already outdated buildings. But most improved in several respects during the inter-war period. Classes at last became smaller. In 1922 there were still 5,000 elementary classes in England and Wales with over 60 children; nearly 3,000 others held between 50 and 60 pupils. By 1935 there were 6,000 classes with over 50 but only 56 with over 60 children. In 1939 only 2,000 classes in the country held over 50.

The movement away from town centres (see Chapter 6) helped to bring down the size of classes. New schools serving the housing estates relieved the pressure on the old urban schools. Relief came, too, from the provision of special classes for the physically handicapped and educationally subnormal. Fisher's Act directed local authorities to discover such children and cater for their needs. The new school medical service was often instrumental in diagnosing if not curing defective eyesight. Teaching was therefore an easier task in smaller classes no longer held back by children demanding specialised attention. And the teachers themselves were better qualified. Not only did the standardised Burnham scale of salaries attract recruits of better quality, but training courses were now obligatory.

Teaching Methods

Elementary teaching methods were formal. Alphabet, mathematical tables and chunks of nineteenth century poetry were learnt by heart and chanted by the class. Teachers drummed facts into their pupils' heads by repeating them several times, then writing them on the blackboard. The method became known as "talk and chalk." It involved little participation or discussion, and scant attention to the individual child. Similarly, music meant singing in chorus—mainly hymns and patriotic songs, especially on 24th May, Empire Day. The only physical exercise was drill, the children bending their knees and stretching their arms in unison.

Discipline was given top priority. As late as 1935 an educationist wrote proudly that "A visitor to one of our elementary schools today will observe the economy and efficiency of its discipline, will note its atmosphere of orderliness and precision." But while better conditions and

Opposite top. A new elementary school in Derbyshire capable of being turned into an open air school. School buildings generally improved in the period.

Opposite bottom. A nature lesson in a London park. Lessons got more interesting as teachers became less obsessed with discipline.

teaching were bringing better health and stricter discipline, other ideals gradually surfaced. In 1921 one of Sir Henry Hadow's committees produced a report on *The Teaching of English in England*. It recommended that "Above all the children should discover the delight of books." A report on Wales suggested that more books should be published in Welsh so that children could actually read in their own language.

Reading ability was increased by the introduction of electric light to the classroom. Some local authorities followed the example of the London County Council in providing warm lighted rooms in the evening where children from less well off homes could do their homework and read on their own. At home their main reading was comics like *Gem* and *Rainbow*. Their favourite fictional character was Billy Bunter of Greyfriars School featured in the *Magnet*. In the later thirties the best sellers were *Dandy* and *Beano*. It is doubtful whether the middle class taste for A. A. Milne's *When We were Very Young* (1924), *Now We are Six* (1927) and *Winnie the Pooh* (1927) or for the books of Kenneth Graham and Beatrix Potter permeated down the social scale. Nevertheless the reading habit was growing. Gradually pupils in school were taught how to gain information themselves from books instead of by passive subjection to the "talk and chalk" methods.

Lessons became more interesting as teachers were less obsessed with the problem of discipline. Radio and films were introduced into the classroom. In the thirties Mary Somerville ran the Schools Broadcasting department of the B.B.C. Local authorities made grants for the purchase of radios and B.B.C. pamphlets so that by 1939 11,000 elementary schools were "listening in." The British Film Institute, founded in 1933, encouraged the making of educational films. Specialised firms hired out projectors and copies of nature films like *Tawny Owl* or historical documentaries such as *Medieval Villages*.

So great was the new emphasis on active participation, however, that radio and films were used less in British schools than in the United States or the U.S.S.R. More popular were visits to parks, museums, factories and castles. The war had encouraged this development. A Board of Education report of 1915 had noted one effect of the shortage of school accommodation immediately after the war: "By curtailing instruction it concentrates the efforts of teachers and scholars in essential matters. Further, the half day out of school has sometimes been used to excellent purpose for physical exercises, swimming, open air work, excursions, visits to museums and galleries and the like." Geography and nature study lessons took place on the hills where contours could be paced out and in parks where pond life and plants could be studied. Classroom walls were hung with pupils' sketches, charts and posters of their travels instead of the old royal portraits. A 1931 report on *The Primary School* announced that the curriculum should be "thought of in terms of activity and experience rather than of knowledge to be acquired or facts to be stored" and should rely "less on mass instruction and more on the encouragement of the individual and group work."

In the infant school, the first two years of the primary school, similar new theories were seeping through. Tiny children were no longer sat in desks and expected to learn the three "R"s but were given water and sand to play with. Free activity and expression slowly became the order of the day. The influence of Froebel, the Macmillan sisters and William James, who believed there should be "no impression without expression," was to revolutionise both nursery and infant schools.

Learning by rote was, however, encouraged by the character of the examination for free places at the state-aided, maintained or new local authority secondary schools. As a condition of their grants from the Board of Education the schools were bound to offer a certain number of these places. Therefore, primary schools in reorganised areas were geared to "the scholarship." They had one main aim: to push as many children as possible through this competitive examination which was stiff but limited in scope. Any child whose parents could afford the fees might gain his place by taking a less stringent examination based on general knowledge rather than achievement in English grammar and arithmetic. Occasionally the Board of Education complained that heads of schools were not filling their quota of free places. In 1922 an Inspector criticised Miss Bell, headmistress of Sutton High School for Girls, for rejecting seven out of nine applicants for these places. Having seen both their examination papers and those of the fee-payers he reported that "a lower standard has been accepted by Miss Bell for fee-payers than for free-placers of the same age." Passing the scholarship was the only way a child of poor parents could hope for secondary education. Any idea that secondary education should be freely available for all received a setback in 1933: free places were subjected to a means test and became known as "special places."

Secondary Education

Demand for education after fourteen was increased by Fisher's introduction of the National School Certificate. An educationist pointed out

If your parents were rich your chances of secondary education were very much higher than if they were poor. A *Punch* cartoon of 1920 by Townsend.

Fond Parent (who has done pretty well in woollens). "Well, Sonny, we've decided to give you the best education that money can buy. After all, you won't have to do anything except be a gentleman."

in 1937 that "The tendency of industry and commerce to regard the possession of the certificate as a *sine qua non* for all recruits to their businesses has often been a potent factor in causing parents to demand the provision of a local secondary school." The building of new secondary schools did not keep up with this demand. Only just over one hundred were put up during the twenties. Plans for more were curbed by the 1931 financial crisis. But the new housing estates did get their schools; others were improved and extended. The extra vacancies, together with Fisher's recommendation to local authorities to provide more free places, did increase the opportunity of the elementary school child from a poor family. In 1914 his chance of reaching secondary school was one in 40; by 1929 it was one in 13. Even this figure varied according to the wealth and generosity of the local authority. Opportunities varied most markedly within the London boroughs. In 1926 one school in Lewisham won as many scholarships as the whole of Bermondsey put together.

Saddest of all were those children who won scholarships and could not take them up. Their parents could not sacrifice the £1 a week they might bring home by leaving school at the earliest opportunity. The children could do nothing to help pay their own way: Fisher's Act had put an end to paid work during term time; unemployment made it difficult to find holiday jobs. No doubt some children sympathised with their parents' view. Orwell wrote in 1937 that "There is not one working class boy in a thousand who does not pine for the day when he will leave school. He wants to be doing real work, not wasting his time on ridiculous rubbish like history and geography." Attempts to raise the school leaving age were not helped by these attitudes of parents and pupils. There was no public pressure to forward the educationists' efforts. In fact there was a strong pressure group against the raising of the leaving age: the Catholics were unwilling to go to the expense of enlarging their schools to cope with the extra year and so feared they would lose pupils. But the greatest stumbling block was money. Fisher's Act allowed local authorities to introduce a leaving age of fifteen, but very few had the resources to do so. Nor could Trevelyan, the President of the Board of Education, find the money for the necessary places and teachers in 1924. When he decided to raise the age in 1929 in order to take half a million young people off the labour market he was foiled by the Catholic peers in the House of Lords. Two years later the slump brought cuts in all spending and made any such legislation impossible. At last Parliament agreed in 1936 that the leaving age should be raised to fifteen on 1st September, 1939. The outbreak of war was even more effective than parsimony or the Catholics in frustrating legislation. The leaving age was not raised until 1947.

Meanwhile the majority of children started work at fourteen. In 1923 only one in eight received full time education after leaving elementary school; by 1931 reorganisation under the Hadow recommendations had raised the figure to one in five. Half the children in secondary schools had free local authority places or county scholarships.

If anything, the secondary schools were too rigidly academic. They were as geared to the school certificate as elementary schools to the "scholarship." If a pupil passed his "school cert." exams in English, mathematics, Latin or science, a foreign language and two other subjects,

he reached the basic standard required to register at a university and thereby gained matriculation exemption. Good grammar schools and ambitious parents expected their children to "get their matric." Many left school after obtaining school cert. or matric. Other students stayed on in the growing number of sixth forms to take the Higher School Certificate and then perhaps compete for university scholarships. The plums were the two hundred state scholarships granted by the Board of Education after 1920. They covered expenses as well as fees. Local authority grants not only varied from place to place but were only paid out after the student had passed the university entrance exam and paid his fees for the first term.

Preparatory Schools

It was therefore extremely difficult for a grammar school boy to get to university. Only 6 out of every 100 managed to do so. If a boy was not lucky enough to win a state scholarship his parents were unlikely to be able to afford to supplement an inadequate local authority grant. If they were wealthy enough to do so they had probably educated their son privately. He went at seven to a fee paying preparatory school. This would often be owned by a retired colonel or major who had found himself unemployed after the war and bought a country house in the southern counties from a family no longer able to afford its upkeep. He and his wife ran the school with the help of assistant teachers often as untrained as themselves and therefore willing to accept low salaries. Paul Pennyfeather, hero of Evelyn Waugh's *Decline and Fall*, was paid £90 a year. Background and family were considered more important for teaching the sons of the privileged classes than any qualifications. As Cyril Connolly, the critic, discovered at his preparatory school, boys were taught that "character is more important than intellect."

Public Schools

Pennyfeather is told by another master that at prep. school "One goes through four or five years of perfect hell at an age when life is bound to be hell anyway, and after that the social system never lets one down." Public school at thirteen was the next rung of the social system for boys. Many were very old foundations. Winchester and Eton dated from the fifteenth century; Harrow, Rugby, Shrewsbury, Westminster and Charterhouse from Tudor and Stuart times. Wellington, Epsom and Marlborough were founded in the nineteenth century. The twentieth now produced Stowe in 1923 and Bryanston in 1928. These new schools adopted some of the traditions but not all the archaic practices of the older foundations such as fagging. Some left tradition even further behind: for example, A. S. Neill at Summerhill and Bertrand and Dora Russell at their progressive school believed in complete freedom of expression, equality between pupil and teacher and no disciplinary action. This was in contrast to the hierarchical attitudes and structure of the older public schools. Cyril Connolly described in *Enemies of Promise* how, at Eton, he was "broken under the strain of beatings at night and bullying by day; all we could hope for was to achieve peace with seniority and then start beating in our turn."

Universities

At public school games were given priority. Any artistic interest tended to be derided. Connolly found that "Boys at Eton wanted one thing, popularity, and the flaw in the Eton education was that work was unpopular." Not every public school was as extreme in its outlook as Eton; and while hard work was despised, ability to gain scholarships to Oxford

In 1920 Oxford University allowed women to take degrees. A woman undergraduate in her study.

and Cambridge was honoured. If a public schoolboy did not win a scholarship he could go to Oxbridge as a commoner so long as his father could pay the high fees. Although the older universities were no longer regarded as playgrounds for wealthy sons, a few undergraduates kept up the old traditions, did little work and were content with mere pass degrees. It was this minority who formed the more eccentric societies and attracted adverse publicity to the universities. In 1921 Oxford's Hide and Seek Club held meetings in and out of the houses of professors; members of Cambridge's Pavement Club, in disapproval of the fast pace of modern life, spent their time on the kerbside playing tiddly winks and marbles. They had little in common with the few grammar schoolboys they met who had worked hard for their state scholarships and went on working hard for their honours degrees. Very often these undergraduates never quite lost their sense of inferiority towards their more privileged contemporaries. Typical of them was Aldous Huxley's character in *Point, Counter Point*: Frank Illidge, dining at a Whitehall Club, "thought again how extraordinary it was, how almost infinitely improbable that he should be sitting there, drinking claret, with the Perpetual Secretary of the British Academy two tables away and the second oldest Judge of the High Court just behind him."

Illidge was ashamed of his working class origins. Many like him blamed these origins if they could not find jobs and tried to hide them if they did achieve success. Ironically the Hadow Report had ensured that the education system would perpetuate these class differences. Because the school leaving age remained as low as fourteen, the break in schooling had to be made at eleven in primary schools in order to provide three years of secondary education. As the break in private schools was at thirteen there was little possibility of any child crossing the barrier between the two school systems during his school years.

Oxford and Cambridge made some attempt between the wars to shed their medieval traditions. In 1920 they agreed to a Royal Commission to look into their efficiency in exchange for a share of the funds of the University Grants Committee which had been set up in 1911. Non-teaching fellowships were abolished; more stringent conditions were laid down for the appointment of dons who now had to retire at sixty-five. Greek was abolished as a compulsory subject in the preliminary examinations. As a further recognition that not all undergraduates would necessarily have had a classical public school education Oxford introduced in 1921 a Modern Greats degree of philosophy, politics and economics. The previous year the university had even allowed women to take degrees. Cambridge did not follow suit until 1945 although women had previously been allowed to study and attend lectures.

Less than one child in every thousand at elementary school could hope to finish his education at Oxford or Cambridge. There were other universities. London was the largest: its colleges were brought under a central administration when Senate House was built in 1929. With so many young soldiers returning from the war there was a demand for university places in 1918. Another character in *Point, Counter Point* commented that "the rush to books and universities is like the rush to the public house." Even so between the wars only one university, Reading, was added to the older provincial universities like Bristol, Nottingham, Manchester, Leeds and Cardiff. Three university colleges were created at Swansea, Leicester and Hull. By 1931 there were only 30,000 under-graduates in England and Wales where $5\frac{1}{2}$ million children were at primary school. Nevertheless, by 1934 a third of the country's under-graduates came from the grammar schools. And in Scotland the uni-versities were more accessible. This was partly because learning was held in higher esteem and was considered worth the loss of a few years' earnings; partly because of the American industrialist Andrew Carne-gie's generous bequests to poor students.

Adult Education

Adults wanted to educate themselves as well as their children. Improved secondary schools turned out more adolescents who enjoyed reading and finding out information for themselves. As working hours were cut back in the late 1930s more time was available for leisure. Longer evenings could be spent at adult education classes as well as at the cinema or listening to the radio. The Workers' Educational Association doubled the number of its pupils between 1920 and 1930. Previously the demand had come from small groups connected with working class organisations. They were more interested in social questions, economics and political problems than in general culture. Now pupils wanted lectures in philo-sophy, archaeology and literature. These subjects were studied, too, at the Women's Institutes, sharing the curriculum with jam making and hygiene. The idea of the Institute had developed in Canada and was brought to England during the war by Mrs. Arthur Watt. In the twenties and thirties branches were opened all over the country, especially in

There was a thirst for adult education after the war. The Women's Institute helped satisfy it by teaching a large number of subjects, such as woodwork (right).

small towns and villages. On the new housing estates fortunate enough to have community centres, groups organised their own classes. It was not until 1944 that the Board of Education made local authorities responsible for these centres.

The radio, like evening classes, satisfied the growing appetite for knowledge. Lord Reith's B.B.C. really was an educator. It broadcast not only talks on books and plays (see Chapter 4) but on psychology, politics and international affairs. Most important of all in spreading knowledge was the paperback book. In 1935 Allen Lane published his first two Penguins, a study of Shelley called *Ariel* by André Maurois and Ernest Hemingway's *A Farewell to Arms*. Recent publications and then older classics became available to the public at 6d. (2½p.) each. Blue non-fiction Pelicans soon followed the orange Penguins. They brought a large public into touch with the current work of scientists, astronomers and economists. The twenties and thirties were exciting years in these fields. Rutherford at Cambridge was attempting to split the atom. The feat was achieved at last by Sir John Cockcroft after P. M. S. Blackett had discovered the electron and Sir James Chadwick the neutron in 1932. Astronomers Sir James Jeans and Sir Arthur Eddington were adding to existing knowledge about the universe; biologists J. B. S. Haldane and Julian Huxley about the human body. For a few pence the public could, after 1935, learn about their discoveries. Sir James Jeans' *The Universe around Us* (1929) and *The Mysterious Universe* (1930) were not too difficult for the layman to understand. Nor were Huxley's *Essays in Popular Science* (1926) or G. D. H. Cole's *Practical Economics*. Thanks to Allen Lane they all became available in paperback editions.

The newly literate public demanded and devoured more print every year. The monthly journal *Discovery*, describing advances in science, archaeology, economics and politics, appeared in 1920. A new edition of the *Encyclopedia Brittanica* was brought out in 1929 and had a great sale. That same year the weekly publication *The Listener* began to make radio talks available in print. Readership of the weeklies was at its highest. *Time and Tide* was founded in 1920; in 1931 the *New Statesman* took over *The Nation*. In 1937 Victor Gollancz's Left Book Club brought hardback as well as paperbacks and weeklies within the scope of the working man's pocket. The club produced a book a month, designed to counteract the influence of fascism. Some publications were mere propaganda; others introduced writers like George Orwell and Arthur Koestler to the 60,000 members. This was nearly double the number of undergraduates in the country. Literacy was increasing at a faster rate than educational opportunities.

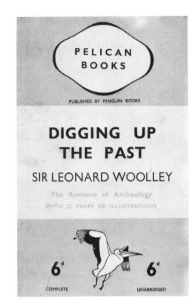

The layman could read about the latest discoveries in Pelican paperbacks. Note the price— 2½p. in today's decimal currency.

8 Left and Right

Fear of Revolution

THERE IS NO DOUBT about the strength of class barriers in the early twenties. Mass entertainment, mass production, slightly improved educational opportunities had not yet begun to break them down. A man's position in society could be placed exactly: his clothes, his diet, his house, his education and his leisure pursuits all gave him away. There is also no doubt that workers were often exploited by employers who cut wages and lengthened the working day as it suited them. In the bad years of the post-war slump there might well have been class warfare.

The employers certainly feared such a revolutionary situation, as did many in government. At a cabinet meeting to discuss the threat of a miner's strike in 1923 the Postmaster General, Sir Laming Worthington Evans, told his colleagues: "We need eighteen battalions to hold London. There are four battalions in Silesia. They could be brought back at once." The previous year Bonar Law had assured his Cabinet that "The stockbrokers are a loyal and fighting class." Many feared that the coming of the first Labour Government in 1924 would bring a revolutionary era. King George V confided his worries to his diary after the new Prime Minister, Ramsay MacDonald, had been to kiss hands: "Today 23 years ago dear Grandmama died. I wonder what she would have thought of a Labour government." There were fears that the army and civil service would be subverted, even marriage abolished. The *English Review* wrote: "For the first time in her history the party of revolution approach their hands to the helm of the state not only, as in the seventeenth century, for the purpose of overthrowing the crown or of altering the constitution but with the design of destroying the very basis of civilised life."

But there was no revolution. The miners swallowed the humiliation of Black Friday. The General Strike merely interrupted the truce between the classes. Middle class strike breakers were more interested in the lark of driving a bus than in keeping the workers down (see Chapter 2). In fact the class battle was never drawn up. For one thing, the general position of wage-earners was improving in spite of the post-war slump. Because prices fell even more than wages there was actually an increase of real income per head; moreover, by 1925 the working class as a whole was receiving more in unemployment insurance and other benefits than it was paying out in taxes. This did not help the plight of the individual means-tested family during the Depression; but in the twenties it did soften class resentment. So, according to Orwell, did the availability of

Opposite. Members of the first Labour government, 1924. Left to right: Ramsay MacDonald, J. H. Thomas and Arthur Henderson. Contrary to many people's fears, the two Labour governments between the wars did not start a revolution in Britain.

inexpensive consumer goods. In *The Road to Wigan Pier* he wrote that "Whole sections of the working class who have been plundered of all they really need are being compensated, in part, by cheap luxuries which mitigate the surface of life. . . . It is quite likely that fish-and-chips, art-silk stockings, tinned salmon, cut-price chocolate, the movies, the radio, strong tea and the Football Pools have between them averted revolution."

The classes did not take up entrenched political positions. While the Labour Party was predominantly middle class, the unions were never revolutionary. Many workers were sympathetic towards Russia: in 1920 the London dockers went on strike rather than load arms onto the *Jolly George* to be used by Poland against the U.S.S.R. But they did not identify themselves as a political group by voting either Labour or for the new British Communist party. In fact over half the population never voted in elections at all. Political apathy was another reason why a revolution could not have taken place in Britain in the twenties. Few showed interest in public affairs. Indifference to the raising of the school leaving age by legislation was typical of the attitude towards Parliament. In 1922 Charles Masterman wrote: "England is not interested in anything at all. It cares nothing about local, municipal or parliamentary politics. It is like a sick man resting after a great outletting of blood. The nervous system is dead. It can only respond to the strongest of stimulants."

The stimulus to increased political awareness came from abroad, from Russia, Spain and Germany. The ideas behind the Bolshevik revolution seemed to offer a challenge to those in power in Britain. Russia herself was not feared as a military power; but communism became the bogey of the ruling classes in the early twenties. Not only did it bring exaggerated fear of the workers: MacDonald's government was forced to resign after dropping a prosecution against a communist, J. R. Campbell, under the Incitement to Mutiny Act of 1797. A letter, probably forged, from Zinoviev, the President of the Communist International, to the British Communist Party suggesting various seditious activities may have helped the Labour Party to lose the following election. In 1925 the Home Secretary, William Joynson Hicks, directed the prosecution of twelve leading communists whom he suspected of inciting union members to strike.

Many intellectuals—for example, the writer Christopher Isherwood (left) and poet W. H. Auden (right) —favoured communism in the thirties.

Intellectuals and Politics

So great a fear of communism was unfounded. The ideology appealed mainly to middle class intellectuals. Their social conscience was aroused by the plight of the unemployed. As the hunger marchers passed through Oxford they were joined by dons and undergraduates whose immediate predecessors had travelled to London on a very different mission to help break the General Strike. At its famous debate in February, 1933, the Oxford Union—the university debating society—resolved it would "in no circumstances fight for its King and Country." This was not so much a vote against war as against unquestioning patriotism: "Your King and Country Need You" had been the recruiting slogan of 1914–18.

Instead of the aesthetics so popular in the twenties, intellectuals began during the thirties to discuss politics. Strong pressures at home and

The so-called Zinoviev Letter first appeared in the *Daily Mail* (left). It was used to create an anti-communist scare, in which Communist and Labour Party supporters were lumped together and branded as "Reds." Notice that Zinoviev is accused of being a German Jew called Apfelbaum.

abroad encouraged extremism. If they were radical they tended to become communists. As Wyndham Lewis pointed out in his *Doom of Youth* in 1932, "The solitary and unique way of being radical that the Anglo-Saxon has . . . is to be communist. Communist, more or less, he must therefore be for there is no other organisation in sight." The poet Robert Graves said that, amongst undergraduates, "the test of being 'advanced' was no longer whether one understood modernist poems, but whether one understood Marxism." Sympathy with Russian communism became fashionable among people who knew little of the dictatorship and purges actually taking place in Russia. They pointed out that it was only non-capitalist Russia which escaped the Depression of 1931. They refused to believe the anti-Soviet propaganda in the press, reading instead the pro-communist propaganda put out by the Left Book Club. John Strachey's *The Coming Struggle for Power* was especially influential. The poets W. H. Auden, Christopher Isherwood and Stephen Spender brought their work together in the anthology *New Signatures* in 1932. Unhappy with the situation at home, they believed that Russia was offering an alternative social organisation for the future. Other writers, equally dissatisfied and disillusioned, went to the other extreme: Hillaire Belloc, G. K. Chesterton, D. H. Lawrence, Eliot and Yeats all adopted right-wing views.

But the middle class intellectuals, left or right wing, were not actively involved in British politics. Their contribution was the myth of an idealised Russia rather than any revolutionary leadership. They preached to each other instead of to the workers. Communism never became a popular movement in Britain. At its peak the Communist Party could only boast 10,000 members; more often it had difficulty in attracting half that number.

Fascism

On the other hand, the British Union of Fascists claimed a membership of 20,000 only eighteen months after its formation in 1932. Its founder, Sir Oswald Mosley, had been given responsibility for dealing with the unemployment situation in the 1929 Labour Government. But MacDonald had rejected his remedies of import controls and public works financed by borrowing. So Mosley resigned. His "New Party" called for the reform of Parliament. Then, disillusioned altogether with the ability of the parliamentary system to cope with the current economic problems, he founded the B.U.F. to advocate the substitution of the corporate state, on the lines of Mussolini's Italy, for parliamentary democracy. The movement had its rich backers, including Lord Rothermere. Publicity was

Supporters of Sir Oswald Mosley's British Union of Fascists salute Mosley at a rally in 1937. The photograph was taken after the B.U.F.'s black uniforms had been banned.

therefore achieved through the *Daily Mail*, the *Evening News* and the *Sunday Dispatch*. It attracted those fearful of the workers and unions, especially ex-army officers. They were joined by members of the lower middle class with a yearning for a romantic leader and by many out-of-work, bored, uneducated youths with a taste for violence, drilling, parades and the uniform of black shirts.

It was by no means certain in the early thirties that these British fascists would not gain as strong a hold as their German and Italian counterparts. There were clashes with the communists which came to a head on 7th June, 1934, at the mass meeting organised by Mosley at Olympia. Eye-witnesses, including Baldwin's private secretary, were shocked at the way the blackshirts beat up the anti-fascist demonstrators. A Conservative M.P. was quoted by the *Yorkshire Post*: "I came to the conclusion that Mosley was a political maniac and that all decent people must combine to kill his movement."

A more serious clash between fascists and communists was only just averted when the blackshirts marched through Bethnal Green in London's East End in October, 1936. Feeling here was particularly high amongst the large Jewish population, because Mosley had whipped up anti-semitic feeling. That March, Herbert Morrison, M.P. for South Hackney, had told the House of Commons about the intimidation of Jews in his constituency: shopkeepers had had windows broken and received murder threats; one man had been in hospital for two weeks after being beaten up. Playwright Bernard Kops, brought up in Stepney, remembers how anti-semitism infected the children who shouted out in the streets "The Yids, the Yids, we've got to get rid of the Yids."

Following the East End disturbances the Public Order Act gave the police power to ban political processions. This affected anti-fascist as well as fascist organisations. But the banning of political uniforms in public was aimed directly at Mosley. Backing from influential people for the B.U.F. was withdrawn gradually after the Olympia meeting. Membership declined as news came from Germany. British writers had watched Hitler's rise to power. Christopher Isherwood described the horrors of early Nazism in *Mr. Norris Changes Trains* and *Goodbye to Berlin*. Graham Greene's novels *Gun for Sale* and *Confidential Agent* had a strong anti-fascist flavour. Even more important, the workers' leaders noticed that Hitler's fascism involved smashing working class organisations like the trade unions and the co-operative movement. British public opinion was shocked by the assassination of the Austrian Chancellor Dolfuss, in 1934.

A scuffle between an onlooker and B.U.F. supporters during a May Day demonstration in Bermondsey, London, 1938.

The Spanish Civil War

Fascism lost support, too, after the outbreak of the Spanish Civil War in July, 1936. General Franco led the army, the supporters of the Catholic hierarchy and the southern landowners in an armed rebellion against the Spanish republican government. Germany and Italy sent arms to Franco, Russia to the Republicans. The National Government in Britain decided on a policy of non-intervention supported by much conservative opinion including the *Daily Mail*, the *Daily Sketch* and the *Observer*. The latter's editor, J. L. Garvin, believed that only the fall of Madrid to

Franco would put an end to communist revolution in Europe. But the majority of the British people were on the other side. Support for the Republicans was not confined to intellectuals and poets. Local Aid Spain Committees were set up in most towns. They held meetings to publicise the Republican cause, collected food, money for medical aid, even soap. The Miners' Federation of Great Britain contributed from its funds and then raised over £80,000 by levying individual members. Most important of all was the formation of the British Battalion of the International Brigade. Of the 2,000 British who volunteered to go to Spain to fight Franco, a large proportion came from the working classes.

Political Stability of Britain

Politics in Britain remained surprisingly stable. While the Liberal Party declined and the Labour Party grew, the National Government ruled throughout the thirties with the support of all moderate opinion. The character of its leaders mirrored the general faith in the constitution and respect for established British methods of government. MacDonald may have been an illegitimate crofter's son but he loved to be entertained by society hostesses. He told the 1930 Labour Party conference that "the system under which we live" was the cause of the Depression, not their politics. But instead of doing anything to beat or alter the system he joined both it and the National Government the following year. Baldwin, too, was more intent on avoiding trouble than imposing any new principles.

Respect for the establishment was deeply ingrained in the majority of the British people. They had been taught at school about the Empire upon which the sun never set and looked at maps showing a quarter of the earth coloured pink. The movement towards self government for India—the Round Table Conferences and negotiations with Gandhi—was attacked by Winston Churchill. He was supported by retired Indian army officers and ex-colonial civil servants living in the home counties and south-coast resorts, by colonial officials home on leave, by businessmen who had served in the colonial branches of their firms, by naval families and by many in the Lancashire towns who believed the prosperity of the cotton industry depended on the Empire markets. But in spite of them, the Empire was beginning to crumble: the Dominions received sovereign status under the Statute of Westminster in 1931; Ireland was on her tortuous way towards independence. All this meant little to working people. Nevertheless, in 1924 and 1925, 27 millions went to the Empire Exhibition at Wembley. They saw an imitation Taj Mahal, watched Burmese dancing girls and walked down Dominion Way and King's Way to get to the funfair.

Ten years later the crowds came out again to celebrate the twenty-fifth year of George V's reign. The public response to the Silver Jubilee celebrations surprised those critics who accused the National Government of a stunt to increase its popularity. Processions and tree plantings were organised by the authorities. But most impressive were the spontaneous demonstrations in the back streets. A London journalist reported that "For miles on end every street was decorated, every house

Queen Mary and George V on Jubilee Day, 1935.

covered with bunting—across the streets festoons hung so closely that one could hardly see the sky." Even those who had little to thank their king and country for during the past twenty-five years joined in. Bernard Kops described how "All those people who I heard screaming against royalty, the tailors and the pressers, many calling themselves red-hot communists, they were all there wildly waving Union Jacks at the passing parade."

Thousands of people sent personal letters of congratulation to the King. They sincerely mourned his death the following year. When his son Edward VIII abdicated before his coronation rather than give up his twice-divorced American fiancée Mrs. Simpson, most ordinary people sympathised with him; but they quickly transferred their loyalty to his brother. Respect and affection for the monarchy remained strong. It was fostered by the B.B.C. The importance of broadcasting in capturing national sentiment was recognised by the Cabinet when it refused to allow Edward to speak to his people before abdicating. Lord Reith had persuaded George V in 1932 to broadcast for the first time. After that the Christmas Day royal talk and *Round the Empire* programme became a national institution. It brought the King into every home. He retained the people's loyalty and affection, becoming a domestic father figure rather than a remote and revered sovereign.

Traditional values remained firmly entrenched, as though the flapper and the shingle had never been. The gay young things settled down to a conventional life in their new semi-detacheds. Galsworthy's Soames of *The Forsyte Saga* became a sympathetic pillar of property and society instead of the pilloried bourgeois originally intended by the author. Nostalgia for stability was apparent in a new craze for Victoriana. Lord Reith—although he had not objected to Edward VIII's proposed broadcast—saw himself and the B.B.C. as the guardian of conventional morality. Its other supporter was the Church. The Archbishop of Canterbury did as much as Baldwin to push Edward off the throne. The King could not possibly be allowed to marry Mrs. Simpson, a divorced woman. Divorce increased during the thirties but still carried a social stigma.

The Prince of Wales, at the Derby in 1921, is saluted by an ex-soldier. He was immensely popular, but his reign as Edward VIII was cut short after he decided to marry a divorced American, Mrs. Simpson.

The wedding of the Duke of
Windsor, ex-Edward VIII, and
Mrs. Simpson, 1937.

The Church

The Established Church retained an influence on the climate of moral
opinion. But it was out of touch with its congregations, more concerned
with its own internal politics and squabbles over the Revised Prayer
Book. Intervention by the Church in everyday life seemed to be confined
to continual denunciations of the growing habits of dancing, pub drinking and going to the cinema. The great exception was William Temple,
Bishop of Manchester, later Archbishop of York, who encouraged youth
organisations and workers' education; as Archbishop of Canterbury
during the coming war he was to involve the Church in the movement
for a fairer society. Meanwhile the current Archbishop of Canterbury,
Randall Davidson, failed to give a strong lead in social matters. During
the General Strike he neither openly supported nor disapproved of
the miners.

But disillusion with the Church had set in before 1926. It was difficult
to reconcile religious faith with the new discoveries of the scientists.
Within the Church the modernists enjoyed a brief success when a defen-
der of evolution, E. W. Barnes, was made Bishop of Birmingham in 1924.

Outside, the Church merely seemed irrelevant. Fewer and fewer people spent their Sunday mornings at worship. Seebohm Rowntree reported in his 1935 survey of York that attendance at church or chapel had dropped by half since 1914, from 35·5 per cent of the population to 17·7 per cent.

The Church of England's lack of appeal left a vacuum for those who needed a faith. Eleven thousand, including writers like G. K. Chesterton and Compton Mackenzie, became Catholic converts. Some joined Frank Buchman's Moral Rearmament group. Buchman had founded the movement in the twenties, giving it the respectable academic name of the Oxford Group. Its aim was to "change" people's lives on the principle that world problems could only be solved by the personal reform of every individual. Others who felt the need for introspection turned to science instead of religion, to a psychoanalyst instead of a priest or Frank Buchman. Sigmund Freud's ideas had been published in Britain before the war but were only widely accepted after 1918. Psychotherapy was used to treat shell-shocked soldiers. It was seriously studied during the twenties. Psychoanalysis became something of a craze amongst women with plenty of time and money.

The thirties were remarkable for national as well as personal introspection. Novelists like J. B. Priestley and sociologists like Seebohm Rowntree became interested in the "condition of England" question. In 1936 sociologist Tom Harrison, poet Charles Madge and film director Humphrey Jennings started Mass Observation. They enlisted people to observe their neighbours' social habits and brought out reports on attitudes to institutions like the pub or special occasions such as the Coronation. It was the beginning of the opinion poll era.

Social Conscience

A new social conscience was apparent in the Penguin political tracts, in the Left Book Club, in the formation of the National Council for Civil Liberties with E. M. Forster as President and in the charitable foundations set up by rich industrialists. An American, E. S. Harkness, founded the Pilgrim Trust in 1930 with an endowment of £2 million to help youth organisations, adult education and especially the unemployed. Lord Nuffield gave Oxford £2 million for the development of a post-graduate medical school and another million for a post-graduate college, Nuffield College, to study the social sciences. He formed a trust endowed with £2 million for improving social conditions in the distressed areas.

Less wealthy individuals also became involved in social work. Middle class volunteers worked for private charitable organisations set up to help the blind, the unmarried mother and the discharged prisoner. They founded and joined organisations to run nursery schools, child and maternity welfare centres and unemployed men's clubs. These voluntary social services often flourished in partnership with state or local authorities. For the government, too, was developing a social conscience. Neville Chamberlain's Unemployment Act of 1934 alleviated some of the horrors of the means test (see Chapter 2) by introducing a uniform system of state control over the local committees. Responsibility for the unemployed was at last being taken by the government. The new attitude to poverty prepared the ground for the Beveridge Report of 1942 and the setting up of the Welfare State. Meanwhile, the 400 branches of the Unemployment Assistance Board were practical evidence, like marketing boards and import quotas, of direct state intervention in everyday life. If there was one great difference between pre-1914 and post-1945 Britain it was the intrusion of the state into individual lives. It brought a vast improvement in the condition of the people.

Pacifism, Sanctions and Appeasement

Social conscience and political awareness were not confined to home. The British were shocked when Japan invaded Manchuria in 1931. They realised that the League of Nations, created after the First World War to prevent future wars by a system of collective security, had failed in its task. Faced with its first threat, the League had done nothing but talk. Many held the British government to be responsible; and many also felt that pacifism, the renunciation of all weapons and war, was the only solution. When the Rev. Dick Shepherd wrote to the press on 16th

October, 1934, asking all those who supported his resolution to "renounce war and never again directly or indirectly support or sanction another," a hundred thousand people replied. They formed the nucleus of the Peace Pledge Union created a few months later at a mass meeting in the Albert Hall.

Pacifism of course made little appeal to the majority; nor could the minority support it in the face of Italy's invasion of Abyssinia in 1935 and Hitler's march into the Rhineland in 1936. Pacifists had to take refuge after all in the idea of collective security and the use of economic and military sanctions to deter an aggressor. This, not peace at any price, was what the majority of voters wanted who took part in the Peace Ballot of 1935 organised by the League of Nations Union. Eleven and a half million people voted. That the ballot was taken seriously and given careful consideration was apparent not only in this figure but in the way its various sections were answered. At the Labour Party conference the same year Ernest Bevin, supporter of the League of Nations' sanctions, attacked George Lansbury's pacifism and won the backing of the Party.

Perhaps few ordinary people realised the full danger of war. Many believed the daily declaration of the *Daily Express* right up until August, 1939, that "There will be no war in Europe this year or next." Nevertheless, the political apathy of the twenties had vanished. When Hitler threatened Czechoslovakia in September, 1938, the British made up their own minds in spite of their rulers and their press. Geoffrey Dawson, editor of *The Times*, wrote on 7th September that the Czechs were wrong to refuse to give up their "fringe alien population who are contiguous to the nation to which they are joined by race." But Dawson was less typical of public opinion than the bus driver who was asked by a Mass Observation interviewer about Chamberlain's visits to Hitler: "What

Chamberlain on his return from Germany, having signed the Munich Agreement. He said "I believe it is peace in our time."

As tension mounted "Anderson" air-raid shelters were distributed (February, 1939).

Slumbering in the sun on Brighton beach in the last few days of peace.

the hell's he got the right to go over there and do a dirty trick like that?" Even before the Prime Minister had agreed with the Fuhrer at Munich that Germany should take over the Sudetenland from the Czechs, the Oxford don, Gilbert Murray was writing to *The Times* to say that "The emotions of the country have seldom been so deeply stirred as by what is called the betrayal of Czechoslovakia."

War

The Munich agreement brought Chamberlain-dolls and sugar umbrellas into the shops and relief tinged with guilt to many people. But the dolls vanished as soon as Hitler repudiated the agreement by marching into Prague the following March. Rearmament in Britain, officially begun in 1935, was now stepped up to a realistic rate. It had already provided sufficient jobs to bring down the numbers of the unemployed. Any belief in collective security as the only alternative to appeasing Hitler and Mussolini was dwindling. The Spanish Republic had fallen in February; the Russians signed a non-aggression pact with Hitler in August. On 1st September the Fuhrer attacked Poland. Two days later Britain declared war on Germany.

The British people who heard the news as they tinkered with their cars or tended their suburban gardens that Sunday morning were already a far more homogeneous nation than they had been in 1918. Improved communications, mass entertainment and production, national newspapers and school examinations had all helped to eliminate regional if not class differences. The pressures of the war years were to increase this trend. The efficient organisation of society necessary in wartime was to help the establishment of the welfare state after the war. The main social problem of the inter-wars had already been solved. The revival of industry through rearmament had ended unemployment and the miseries of the dole. Ironically, one evil of the period had defeated another: the need to fight fascism at last defeated the worst effects of the Depression.

Japanese invade Manchuria (Sept. 18).
Britain goes off Gold Standard (Sept. 21).
Second Round Table Conference (Sept.).
National Government wins election (Oct. 27).
Statute of Westminster (Nov).
Opening of Sadlers' Wells Theatre.
Ford opens Dagenham factory.
First trolley buses in London.

1932 International disarmament conference opens at Geneva (Feb.).
Scientists at Cambridge split atom.
Shakespeare Memorial Theatre opens.
Mosley founds British Union of Fascists.
First test matches between India and England.
London Philharmonic Orchestra formed under Sir Thomas Beecham.
Introduction of Means Test (Oct.).
George V's first Christmas Day broadcast.

1933 Number of unemployed rises to nearly three million (Jan.).
Hitler becomes German Chancellor (Jan. 30).
Oxford Union votes against fighting for King and Country (Feb. 9).
Agricultural Marketing Act fixes import quotas (Mar. 13).
London Passenger Transport Board set up and begins operating tubes,
buses and trams (July 1).
Electric service opens on London–Brighton railway line.

1934 *Queen Mary* launched by Queen Mary.
Disarmament conference adjourned.
Battersea Power Station opened.
Road Traffic Act introduces driving tests.
Fred Perry first wins Wimbledon (July).
George V opens Mersey tunnel (July 18).
Rev. Dick Shepherd's Peace Meeting at Albert Hall (Oct. 16).

1935 Baldwin becomes Prime Minister (June 7).
Result of Peace Ballot organised by League of Nations Union (June 27).
Government of India Act (Aug. 4).
Bevin defeats Lansbury at Labour Party Conference (Oct. 1).
Italy invades Abyssinia (Oct. 4).
National Government wins election (Nov. 14).
Robert Watson Watt demonstrates radar.
William Walton's "First Symphony" played.

1936 Death of George V (Jan. 20).
Edward VIII proclaimed King (Jan. 28).
Germans occupy Rhineland (Mar. 7).
Spanish Civil War begins (July 18).
Jarrow hunger march to London (Oct. 5).
B.B.C. opens television service (Nov. 2).
Public Order Act (Nov.).
Edward VIII abdicates (Dec. 11).

1937 Coronation of George VI (May 12).
Chamberlain becomes Prime Minister (June 28).
A. P. Herbert's private Bill becomes Divorce Act (July).
Daily Telegraph absorbs *Morning Post*.
Southern Ireland becomes Republic of Ireland outside Commonwealth.

1938 German forces occupy Austria (Mar. 11).
May Day rally (May 1) demands lead to Holidays with Pay Act.
Chamberlain meets Hitler at Munich (May 29).

British navy mobilised (Sept. 28).
Germany occupies Sudetenland (Oct. 1).
Queen Elizabeth launched by Queen.
1939 Steel "Anderson" air raid shelters distributed in London (Feb. 25).
Germans enter Czechoslovakia (Mar. 15).
Conscription introduced (July 1).
Trial blackout over half Britain (Aug. 9).
German–Soviet pact (Aug. 23).
Germany invades Poland (Sept. 1).
B.B.C. TV closes down for duration of war (Sept. 1).
Evacuation of children from cities begins (Sept. 1).
Britain and France declare war on Germany (Sept. 3).

Further Reading

A. J. P. Taylor, *English History 1914–1945*, Oxford University Press, 1965; Penguin, 1974.
C. L. Mowat, *Britain between the Wars*, Methuen, 1955.
G. D. H. Cole and Raymond Postgate, *The Common People, 1746–1946*, Methuen, 1938; revised 1946.
Robert Graves and Alan Hodge, *The Long Weekend*, Faber, 1940.
Malcolm Muggeridge, *The Thirties*, Hamish Hamilton, 1940.
John Raymond (ed.), *The Baldwin Age*, Eyre & Spottiswoode, 1960.
James Laver, *Between the Wars*, Studio Vista, 1961.
Marion Bowley, *Housing and the State, 1919–1944*, Allen & Unwin, 1945.
S. J. Curtis, *Education in Britain since 1900*, Andrew Dakers, 1952.
C. W. Cunnington, *English Women's Clothing in the Present Century*, Faber, 1952.
J. B. Priestley, *English Journey*, Heinemann, 1934.

Aldous Huxley, *Point, Counter Point*, 1928.
        Brave New World, 1932.
Evelyn Waugh, *Decline and Fall*, 1928.
        Put out More Flags, 1942.
J. B. Priestley, *The Good Companions*, 1929.
A. G. Macdonell, *England, their England*, 1933.
George Orwell, *The Road to Wigan Pier*, 1927.
        Down and Out in Paris and London, 1933.

Index

Acknowledgements

The publishers and author would like to thank the following for loaning pictures used to illustrate this book: The Radio Times Hulton Picture Library, frontispiece, pp. 6–7, 9 bottom, 11, 14 bottom, 15–17, 19, 21, 23, 26–33, 34 bottom, 37 top, 38–42, 43 top, 44, 48–58, 60, 61 bottom, 62–63, 65, 67, 68 bottom left, 70 top, 72–86, 89, 91–92, 94–100, 105–108, 110, 112, 114–115, 117 top, 118–122; Imperial War Museum, p. 9 top; Victoria and Albert Museum, p. 13; The Kodak Museum, pp. 18, 46, 61 top, 70 bottom, 71; The Mansell Collection, p. 37 bottom; London Transport Executive, pp. 64, 69; British Railways, p. 68 top; The Science Museum, p. 68 middle and bottom; Weidenfeld & Nicolson Ltd., p. 88; The Geffrye Museum, p. 90, jacket and first page of colour; The Trustees of the London Museum, second page of colour; Shell-Mex and B.P. Ltd., third page of colour; A. R. J. Brudenell-Bruce and Michael Parkin Fine Art Ltd., fourth page of colour.